Seeing the Sky

100 Projects, Activities, and Explorations in Astronomy

FRED SCHAAF

with illustrations by Doug Myers

Wiley Science Editions

 JOHN WILEY & SONS, INC.

New York • Chichester • Brisbane • Toronto • Singapore

Library of Congress Cataloging-in-Publication Data

Schaaf, Fred.
  Seeing the sky : 100 projects, activities, and explorations in astronomy / Fred Schaaf.—Wiley science ed.
     p.   cm.
  Includes bibliographical references (p.
  ISBN 0-471-52093-4.—ISBN 0-471-51067-X (pbk.)
    1. Astronomy projects—Popular works. 2. Astronomy—Observers' manuals. I. Title.
  QB64.S427   1990
  523—dc20   89-70673
                                                                            CIP

Printed in the United States of America

90 91 10 9 8 7 6 5 4 3 2 1

Preface

The first stirrings of this book arose out of a desire to motivate myself. My goal was to spark myself to undertake these projects, which I had long contemplated, long known to be intriguing, but had never fully attempted.

My hope now, of course, is that these projects will also inspire others to actual participation. The fact that they are essentially cost-free and original should help spur interest. But there is a further step that I feel is every bit as important as trying the projects: Readers of this book should report their results.

Before I discuss why I think reporting your results is so important and how you may do it, I should first describe further what kind of projects these are.

For the most part, I would characterize the activities or projects here as easy to understand. They are aimed at adult skywatchers, but I think they are accessible to bright students of fairly young age. Of course, how difficult they are lies partly in how carefully and thoroughly you perform them. You will not need Bunsen burners, mass spectrometers, the Space Telescope Wide-Field Planetary Camera Investigation Definition Team Charge-Coupled Device, or a research grant. But you will need a lot of ambition and perseverance and a lot of willingness to stand outdoors on cold nights—things I think you will find in abundance once you get a taste of the beauty and fascination of celestial bodies and phenomena.

Some of these projects are not strictly or directly about *celestial* objects. As in my previous books, I have included a fair serving of sky phenomena like rainbows and halos, which arise in our atmosphere, though usually with the Sun or the Moon as the light sources. These spectacular phenomena have fallen into the crack between astronomy and meteorology, and they deserve attention.

A very few of the projects are ones whose phenomena are rare enough so that you might not even see them this year. (I wonder, though, if we have more people out there looking for them knowledgeably, some of those phenomena may turn out to be far more common than previously imagined.) On the other hand, many of the projects can be performed virtually any week of any year. And some of them are the kinds that you can go on performing again and again, gathering ever more and better information, for as long as you want—which may be a lifetime if you truly catch the infectious spirit of these observations. Within many of the activities are numerous individual projects and questions, so there is certainly enough here to keep any skywatcher joyfully busy for a long time.

These projects would not have been published in anything like their present form without the help of several important people. At Wiley, David Sobel gave advice and assistance from the start to the end of this endeavor. Cathleen McCann did an able job of polishing the manuscript through copyediting, and Laura Cleveland of WordCrafters Editorial Services performed a skillful job of putting the book together.

Now, returning to my earlier point: I would like to urge, as strongly as possible, not only that you the reader try these projects, but also that you report your results. Much of what you find may merely satisfy your own curiosity (which is no small reward), but some of it could be of scientific importance or (more likely) could simply help open new vistas of appreciation and enjoyment for the rest of the skywatchers of the world. Whatever you find, I would like to hear about it and hope to be able to answer some of you. (A self-addressed, stamped business envelope will help!) You can write to me in care of Wiley Science Editions, John Wiley & Sons, Inc., 605 Third Avenue, New York, NY 10158. Perhaps I can advise you on whether you should seek to publish your results yourself. My hope is that many of the results—with your name and full credit—can be published in my future magazine articles and columns or even in a successor to this book.

Whether we publish or not, I want to hear what you learn and share my findings and those of others with you. After all, no single one of us can be awake 24 hours a day or be everywhere to see everything in this nonstop play of the most intricate, intriguing, and sometimes quite literally breathtaking wonders we call the sky. But if a lot of us try the activities in this book and report our findings, perhaps we will move closer to that goal. For we will have formed a network of wonder that will have multiplied our eyes and enhanced our hearts and heads manyfold.

Fred Schaaf

Note on the Measurement of Time, Position, Angular Distances, and Brightness in Astronomy

The following concepts are not necessary to know for most activities in this book; for a few activities, however, they are very important.

Time. Mention is made in Tables 16 and 18 (on eclipses) about Universal Time (UT). This is 24-hour time, essentially the same as Greenwich Mean Time (GMT). The day in UT begins at midnight in the time zone of England's Greenwich meridian. In the United States, Local Standard Time is 5 (Eastern Standard Time [EST]), 6 (Central Standard Time [CST]), 7 (Mountain Standard Time [MST]), and 8 (Pacific Standard Time [PST]) hours behind UT. Thus, 10^h UT on January 18 would be 5:00 A.M. EST, and 4^h UT on January 18 would be 11:00 P.M. EST on January 17.

Position. The system of celestial coordinates most referred to in this book is that of right ascension (RA) and declination. On the celestial sphere of the heavens, with its equator and poles directly over those of Earth, RA and declination are similar to longitude and latitude, respectively, on Earth. RA is not measured in degrees west or east of the Greenwich meridian, however, but in 24 "hours" (containing "minutes" and "seconds" of angular measure), which run east from the 0^h line of RA. That line goes through the vernal equinox point in the sky (where the Sun is located in the heavens as spring begins). Declination is measured in degrees, minutes, and seconds, like latitude, but declinations north of the celestial equator are preceded by a plus sign (+) and those south of the celestial equator, by a minus sign (−).

Angular Distance. From horizon to zenith is 90 degrees (out of the 360 degrees around the entire heavens above and below the horizon). The Moon and Sun appear about 0.5 degree wide. Your fist at arm's length is about 10 degrees wide. Your hand at arm's length, with the forefinger and little finger extended fully, is about 15 degrees.

NOTE ON MEASUREMENT

Brightness. In astronomy, brightness is measured by *magnitude*. Originally all naked-eye stars were categorized in six classes of brightness, from first (brightest) to sixth (faintest). In modern times, the scale has been extended to zero and to negative magnitudes for very bright objects and to much higher numbers for objects so faint that they require optical aid to see. Decimals are used between two magnitudes: A star midway in brightness between magnitude 1.0 and 2.0 is 1.5 (the 1.5 star is dimmer than magnitude 1.0—the lower the magnitude, the brighter the object). A difference of 1 magnitude means one object is about 2.512 times brighter than another. This is because it was considered useful to set a 5-magnitude difference equal to 100 times—2.512 (actually 2.5118...) multiplied by itself 5 times is 100.

Metric Conversions. This book uses both miles and kilometers. To convert from kilometers to miles, multiply the figure by 0.6214. To convert from miles to kilometers, multiply the figure by 1.609.

Contents

CONTENTS

CONTENTS

CONTENTS

RAINBOWS, HALOS, CORONAS, AND GLORIES   143

ECLIPSES   173

ELUSIVE GLOWS   189

CONTENTS

MOON

1.

Moon Maps and Bias

Observe naked-eye lunar surface markings on the waxing gibbous Moon around sunset or on the waning gibbous Moon around sunrise. Draw your own map of these markings, without reference to any other map. Get other people to perform the same task at the same times you do. Finally, categorize the participants according to how much telescopic observation of the Moon or how much viewing of Moon photographs they have previously done, and compare their results.

Drawing your own map of the Moon is a fine introduction to the discipline of careful observation. It is also good as a first lunar activity because later you may become biased from looking at professional Moon maps in preparation for more detailed naked-eye observations of the Moon (such as in Activity 5). Of course, you already may have looked at enough photographs or maps of the Moon or viewed it enough in the past through telescopes to be somewhat biased. But if that is so, you are at least less biased now than you are likely to become.

William Gilbert's moon map (adapted by Doug Myers). Made before Gilbert's death in 1603, this is the only known pretelescopic moon map and the wonder is why it is so inaccurate.

The best method of testing the question of bias is the second part of this activity: to have people with different levels of lunar experience attempt naked-eye moon maps at the same times you do.

Of course, comparing the results of these other mapmakers will throw light on additional interesting questions—for instance, how much more detail on the Moon can be detected by people with especially sharp eyesight? But that inquiry urgently raises an important complication for all who would perform this activity: How does one keep the variables of previous familiarity with the Moon, sharpness of vision, and other factors separate from one another?

You will need to define classifications such as "moderate experience" or "sharp eyesight" as precisely and as near to quantitatively as possible. Some parts of the definitions will be obvious, of course. Has the person ever looked through a telescope at the Moon? Does he or she own a telescope? Does he or she own any astronomy books? Further ideas for improving the definitions with which you begin can lead to much better end results.

There are some other kinds of variables that, fortunately, can be eliminated. Each person should observe and sketch for the same amount of time—perhaps 15 minutes. Even more importantly, each person should observe and sketch at the same time and in the same county or small geographical region (so weather is likely to be the same). The ideal time is when the sky is neither too similar to the Moon's brightness (as in bright daylight) nor too different (as in full night)—in other words, around sunrise or sunset. Joseph Ashbrook suggested that late morning twilight (with waning gibbous Moon) was the best time. See what *you* think.

Questions

1. At what exact time do you have greatest visibility of lunar details? At what time in twilight does visibility improve or worsen the quickest? How much does haze and the Moon's angular altitude affect when these times occur?

2. How much does previous experience with the Moon bias one's drawing of a naked-eye Moon map? How much does the sharpness of one's vision affect the accuracy and amount of detail on such a map?

2.

Features at Each Lunar Phase

Study and draw the Moon's surface features on each day of its entire cycle of phases from one New Moon until the next.

In this activity, the observer takes advantage of the many different lighting angles that features of the Moon undergo at different lunar phases. Some of these features are spectacular only around certain phases, and not even visible at others.

How many days of phases make up the whole cycle? As viewed against the background of stars, the Moon takes about 27⅓ days to complete one orbit of the Earth—a *sidereal month.* But during that time, Earth and Moon are also moving onward in their orbit of the Sun. As a result, a period of roughly 29½ days elapses before Earth, Moon, and Sun are in the same position relative to one another and the same lunar phase recurs. The 29½ days between any phase and its next recurrence is called the *synodic month.*

But where in the cycle of phases should we begin? For a number of reasons, New Moon is the best place to start. Astronomers measure the Moon's "age" each

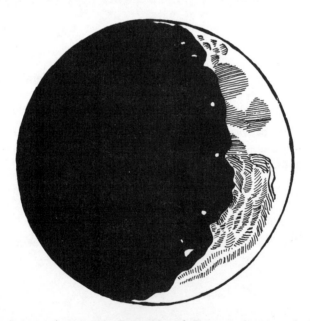

Galileo moon map (adapted by Doug Myers). This was the second of two drawings Galileo made on November 30, 1609, his first two recorded telescopic observations (the magnification was 20 times).

month from the moment of New Moon, the moment of seeming birth. Indeed, the synodic month from one New Moon to the next has a special name. It is called a *lunation.*

Think of the lunation as a series of nightly pictures forming an eternal book that presents all we can ever see of our Moon. That concise and perfect book—one ideal form of organization in time of what the Moon offers—is what we want to produce if we wish to know the Moon.

Actually, of course, a lunation does not offer us quite the perfect series of nightly pictures that our sense of order seeks. For one thing, there are not *exactly* 29 days in a lunation. Also, for at least a day or two around New Moon—and this is variable—the Moon is too slightly illuminated or too near the Sun to view. There is one final important departure from perfection. The best time to look for naked-eye lunar surface features each night—around sunrise or sunset—is not likely to be precisely a whole number of days past the moment of New Moon.

Does the exact age of the Moon matter? Does one-quarter (or three-eighths) of a day make a significant difference in what is illuminated? Sometimes it does, even for naked-eye observers. The reason for this is the special visibility of features at the *terminator*—the line of sunrise or sunset on the lunar surface. Near this line, shadows of rugged lunar topography are longest, the features etched in sharpest relief. High-altitude features (mountains and crater rims) catch the rising sun earlier (and the setting sun later) than low-altitude features (the plains of the lunar "seas" and crater floors). The naked-eye jaggedness of the terminator is most often due to the mountainous edge of a *lunar sea* ("sea" or *mare,* plural *maria*) being in sunlight while when the much lower plain of the sea itself is not. The terminator on the Moon moves at an amazingly slow rate—only about 9 miles per hour, even at the Moon's equator. But multiply that number by 6 hours and you see that one-fourth of a day can indeed bring to light the noticeable start of a huge new lunar feature.

So the practitioner of this activity really should note the time of the lunar observation and calculate to the hour the exact age of the Moon. (Just check any almanac for the precise time of the last New Moon, and figure out how much time has elapsed between then and the observation.)

What other factors cause trouble for our goal of a perfect series of pictures that make up, once and for all, the entire panorama of the lunation? One such factor is libration. This phenomenon is explained and studied in Activity 6. You can ignore libration in your first attempt to draw the features throughout an entire lunation, but you will soon need to learn more about it.

The Moon offers very special sights when you can see it at less than 1 ½ days old or more than 28 days old. These sights are discussed in Activity 12.

Questions

1. At what ages of the Moon do you first and last notice a surface feature? At which ages (if any) do you see one crescent point longer?

2. At what ages of the Moon do you see the most and the least jaggedness of the terminator? What specific features cause the jaggedness? (You may need to use optical aid or refer to Moon maps in books.)

3.

Shades of Bright and Dark on the Moon

Make a chart showing levels of brightness (from brightest to darkest) on the naked-eye Moon. Do this at different phases, noticing the changes in each feature's or each area's brightness caused by the changing angle of illumination from the Sun. Rate the brightness of regions on a 1-to-5 scale or even on a 1-to-10 scale (0 = shadow; 1 = darkest illuminated regions; 10 = brightest regions).

Most of us think of the naked-eye Moon as a bright disk with some dark markings. A careful look shows instead a marvelous range of subtle shadings—and brightenings (that is, areas somewhat brighter than the typically rather bright highlands of the Moon). How can we have overlooked some of these spectacular bright areas? They are only prominent when viewed at the best time of our day (near sunrise or sunset) and at the best time of the Moon's (near the Moon's noon—the phases when the Sun is high in the lunar sky over the areas).

Telescopic observers of the Moon refer to a scale of "degrees" of brightness ranging from 1 to 10 (with 0 for shadow). The floors of the craters Grimaldi and Riccioli are judged darkest of illuminated areas, rating a 1; parts of the crater Aristarchus are the brightest on the Moon, rating a 10.

But the naked-eye study of the Moon's gradations of brightness turns up some new information. The smaller features, visible in telescopes, blend to varying extents to produce quite different appearances of bright and dark. Looking at the Moon with the naked eye gives us new insight into the largest scale distribution of features—in this particular activity, the distribution of the brighter "lunarite" and darker "lunabase" with all that they may mean.

At certain lunar phases, the Sun shines high in the sky over particular young craters and over the bright dust that is strewn out from them in long streaks called *rays*. Whereas such a crater and its vicinity seem quite ordinary at other times, the high Sun lights up its ray system into startling prominence. The relatively small craters Stevinus and Byrgius do not receive much attention, even in many detailed telescopic guides to the Moon. But you will find that the two bright areas of their ray systems are virtually as prominent to the naked eye as the dark maria at the right times (Earth sunset with waxing gibbous Moon for the Stevinus area, Earth sunrise with waning gibbous Moon for the Byrgius area). The Stevinus region looks almost like a bright twin of the famous dark Mare Crisium somewhat north of it.

Questions

1. What bright areas other than those of Stevinus and Byrgius can you identify? At what age of the Moon is each most prominent?

2. What are the brightest and darkest features you see at each phase? Which of the maria seems darkest?

3. Where do you see the most numerous delicate patches of shading on the naked-eye Moon?

4.

Patterns in the Distribution of Lunar Features

Organize the Moon's naked-eye features into as many patterns or systems as possible. Examine patterns and systems already known, but also invent at least a few of your own. Decide which are most useful for memorizing the Moon's layout and which may hold significance for our understanding of the Moon's nature.

Telescopic and spacecraft studies of the Moon have revealed many interesting patterns in the distribution of lunar features. Most remarkable is the extreme dissimilarity in the amount of maria on the near and far sides. Other patterns, maybe of coincidence rather than significance, include the three great hemisphere-spanning "crater-chains" on the Earth-facing side of the Moon and J.E. Spurr's "grid system" of faults and ridges. But what organizations of features might naked-eye study of the Moon reveal?

Naked-eye study lends itself to the recognition of very large-scale patterns. Our previous two activities can be helpful in identifying these patterns in the distribution of brightness or reflectivity (Activity 3) and in topography (Activity 2, noting the irregularities of the Moon's terminator at various phases caused by elevation differences).

The easiest patterns to notice with the naked eye are, of course, simply those of the maria themselves. Best known are the old, fanciful images of earthly things pictured in the maria by various cultures throughout history (and prehistory). However much or little they may stir our imagination, these images can serve a practical purpose by aiding our attempts to memorize the positions of lunar features. They can help you learn your way around the Moon. Of all the old images, the Lady in the Moon may be the most intricate and accurate. Where did Apollo 11 land? Ever so slightly above the small ear of the Lady. Figure 1 shows one version of the Lady in the Moon and three of the other most famous images.

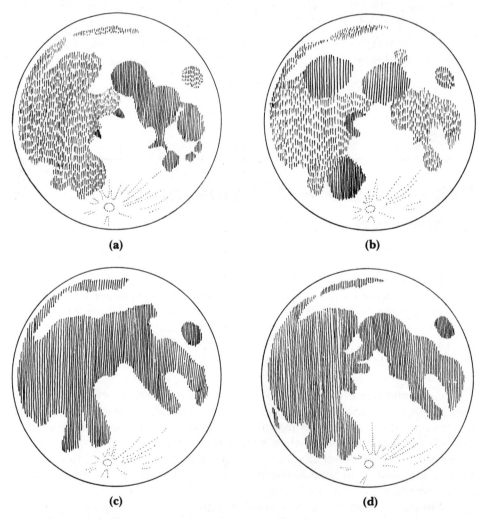

(a) **(b)**

(c) **(d)**

Figure 1 (a) Lady in the Moon; (b) Man in the Moon; (c) Lunar Hare; (d) Lunar Crab.

You can also study the distribution of physically different kinds of maria. At least a few of these distinctions you can see with the naked eye—for instance, the distinction between some of the impact, or "regular," maria and the overflow, or "irregular," maria. You can see the difference between an almost circular ("regular") mare-like Imbrium and a far from circular ("irregular") mare-like Oceanus Procellarum for yourself.

Questions

1. What patterns in the distribution of bright and dark can you identify on your map from Activity 3? What patterns of topographic ruggedness and smoothness can you identify on your maps from Activity 2?

2. Which image in the Moon's markings (such as The Lady in the Moon) do you find most useful for memorizing the placement of lunar features? What benefits do others have? Can you invent your own?

3. Does any pattern in the distribution of maria or other lunar features seem to correlate with lunar latitude, longitude, rotational direction, orbital direction, or orientation to Earth?

5.

Smallest, Most Difficult Naked-Eye Lunar Features

With the naked eye, try to see the smallest, the narrowest, the lowest-contrast, and the otherwise most elusive features you can on the Moon.

No detailed lunar maps are offered in this book because they would possibly bias readers attempting the first two activities. But for the current activity, you will need to prepare carefully for the specific lunar features sought—either with optical aid or, if you have none, and we are to obey this book's imperative of no expense, with lunar maps and photographs available in many books at your local library.

The following are notes to aid in this activity. You might be the first person ever to glimpse a few of these features with the naked eye and to know what you are seeing! Sharp eyesight is an advantage, but knowledge and perseverance are very

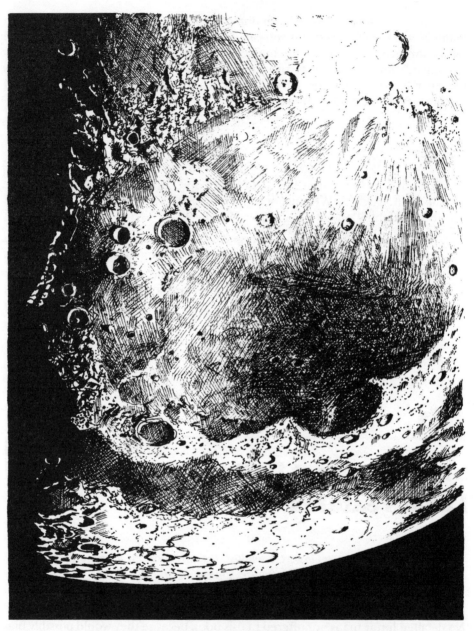

Mare Imbrium region, including Apennines, at terminator.

important, too. So are sky conditions. Make sure to observe as high a Moon as possible, as near as possible to our dusk or dawn time of maximum lunar feature visibility.

Maria. In my previous book, *The Starry Room,* I discussed W. H. Pickering's 1 to 12 scale of lunar features increasingly difficult to glimpse with the naked eye, and I provided an identification chart for the features. On Pickering's scale, Mare Nectaris is rated 2 and Mare Humorum is rated 3—quite easy for average eyesight under good conditions. These maria are not much more than 200 miles across. Mare Humorum is roughly the area of England, New York State, or two of the Great Lakes put together—rather small regions to be seen easily from up to 250 million miles away. But most of us should be able to detect slightly smaller features directly and much smaller features indirectly. Numbers 7 and 9 on Pickering's scale are the smaller Mare Vaporum and Sinus Medii. I feel that Sinus Medii is easier to see than Pickering's rating suggests.

How many of the Moon's maria can unaided vision perceive? At least 11 of the maria, according to my count. Table 1 lists them and suggests a few more bays and lakes to try—plus Mare Australe, which sometimes just peeks around the lunar limb.

Table 1
Maria and similar formations
potentially visible to the naked eye

Oceanus Procellarum (Ocean of Storms)

Mare Imbrium (Sea of Rains)

Mare Serenitatis (Sea of Serenity)

Mare Tranquilitatis (Sea of Tranquility)

Mare Fecunditatis (Sea of Fertility)

Mare Crisium (Sea of Crises)

Mare Nubium (Sea of Clouds)

Mare Vaporum (Sea of Vapors)

Mare Nectaris (Sea of Nectar)

Mare Humorum (Sea of Moisture)

Mare Frigoris (Sea of Cold)

Sinus Medii (Central Bay)

Sinus Aestuum (Bay of Heats)

Lacus Somniorum (Lake of Dreams)

Sinus Roris (Bay of Dews)

Palus Epidemiarum (Marsh of Epidemics)

Mare Australe? (Southern Sea)

Mountain Ranges. Individual mountains on the Moon are too small to see with the naked eye (except indirectly in a rare *grazing occultation* of a bright star or planet; see Activity 9). But can the mightiest of Mare Imbrium's ramparts, the 500-mile-long Apennines range, be seen with the naked eye? If one means the entire strip of highland area, which their peaks dominate, then certainly yes. By that definition, several other mountain ranges also can be seen—perhaps even the Riphaeus Mountains (12 on Pickering's scale, his most difficult object). But there is a more dramatic way to detect the Apennines—by the deformation they make in the terminator! Just after First Quarter, the Apennines catch Sun long before the surrounding regions and cast 100-mile-long shadows. Almost 2,000 years ago, Plutarch suggested the Moon must have mountains and valleys, and the Apennines' altering of the terminator may have been his clue.

Craters. The crater Clavius forms a naked-eye notch on the terminator. Its walls rise over 12,000 feet, and its diameter is about 145 miles (the latter second only on the Moon's near side to the far more foreshortened Bailly). What other craters might be seen with the naked eye in the same way? The region around Copernicus sticks out dramatically at the terminator a few days after First Quarter—but can one really detect the crater itself in this way? Another prime candidate is Ptolemaeus, 90 miles across and rimmed with elevations as high as 9,000 feet.

Might a lunar crater be seen directly far from the terminator? Most have light floors that do not contrast enough with the surrounding highlands. The 120-mile-wide Grimaldi has an extremely dark floor, but it is quite near the limb except at a favorable libration. One last crater, also rather dark floored, deserves mention: Plato. Is the highland area surrounding it wide enough to give it a good background for a naked-eye glimpse? Unfortunately, Plato is only 60 miles wide—perhaps it deserves to be number 13 on Pickering's scale of 12!

Questions

1. How many maria, mountain ranges, and ray systems can you detect with the naked eye ? Can you detect craters on the terminator or far from it?
2. Is there any valley, cliff, ray, or rill on the Moon wide enough to see with the naked eye? If not, how little optical aid suffices?

6.

Libration

Learn about libration by sketching the shape and position of naked-eye lunar features near the Moon's limb, especially Mare Crisium, several times a month. Note also what lunar features are reached by the terminator at certain "ages" of the Moon each month.

Because the Moon rotates in the same amount of time it revolves (orbits) around Earth, it always keeps approximately the same face pointed toward us—but not *exactly* the same face. The various tiltings of the Moon's face are examples of *libration*. And these tiltings can often be noticed by the naked-eye observer who knows what to look for.

Libration brings into sight a little of the Moon's surface past the Moon's north or south pole and a little past what we can normally see of the western or eastern edges. Because of libration, we get to view about 59 percent of the Moon's surface, rather than the 50 percent we would expect. But what the naked-eye viewer notices is change in apparent shape and position of large lunar features a bit farther in than the mean edge.

Most attention-grabbing of these features is Mare Crisium. It lies fairly near the preceding edge of the Moon in the latter's journey across our sky, so it is observable from just after New Moon to just after Full Moon. What is Mare Crisium's appearance at opposite extremes of libration? This actually circular mare varies from appearing to be a thin, dark line at the very edge to a fairly fat oval comfortably well in from the edge.

The simplest version of our activity would be merely to draw the appearance of Mare Crisium on the Moon at various times. But the additional questions below pose further challenges. Moreover, you should soon find yourself wanting to know why and when libration occurs.

Actually, the term *libration* is applied to several different kinds of motions with different causes. Of the four major types, two of them (*physical libration* and *diurnal libration*) are too slight to notice with the naked eye. On the other hand, the *libration in latitude* has an easily visible effect, showing almost 7 degrees past the Moon's north pole, then about the same amount past the Moon's south pole half an orbit later. Its explanation lies in the fact that the Moon's polar axis is inclined almost 7 degrees to the plane of its orbit. The *libration in longitude* usually shows up to 6 degrees, but sometimes nearly 8 degrees, past the mean eastern and western lunar limbs. It occurs because the Moon rotates at essentially a constant rate but travels around the Earth at varying speed (fastest when closest, slowest when farthest) due to the Moon's non-circular orbit. Figure 2 shows how this enables us to see sometimes farther beyond the edge of the Moon that leads in its orbital journey and sometimes farther beyond the edge of the Moon that trails in that journey.

Of course, at any given time what we see is a combination of the librations. It

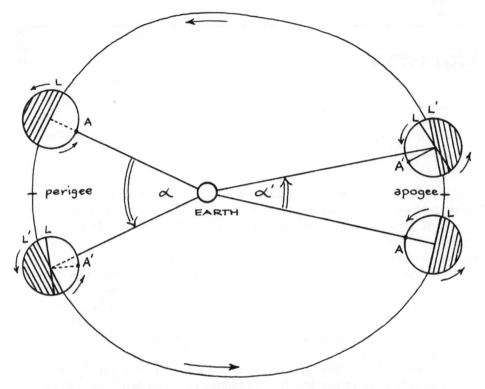

Figure 2 Cause of the Moon's libration in longitude. Although the two angles are different, the Moon travels through them in the same amount of time because it is moving faster near perigee. Consequently, the point A, exactly on the line connecting the Earth's and the Moon's centers, falls behind or ahead, permitting the lunar regions between L and L' on either edge of the Moon to become visible.

used to be that one had to look up the *selenographic latitude and longitude* of the Earth to figure the extent of the two major librations for a certain night. Since its July 1978 issue, however, *Sky & Telescope* has used a computer program by John Westfall each month to provide a clearer single figure for the combined direction and extent of the major librations. That issue also has several excellent articles on libration, including one by a naked-eye observer who discovered these motions for himself.

Questions

1. What are the different shapes and positions of Mare Crisium from week to week, month to month? What other naked-eye features show interesting variations due to libration?

2. How does what features appear on the terminator at certain "ages" of the Moon vary as a function of libration?

7.

Size of the Moon

Compare the Moon with a dime at arm's length and with small star groupings in order to find how much we typically overestimate its size. Then, keep detailed records of how much larger than usual it seems when it is near the horizon on different occasions. See if you can determine how much your body's orientation, the sky conditions, and having distant earthly objects in your view affect your perception of the Moon's size.

We have an understandable tendency to overestimate the size of so bright and striking a Moon high in our sky. On the other hand, our perception that the low Moon is especially huge—the famous Moon Illusion—has complex causes and remains imperfectly explained. Indeed, our understanding of why the Moon appears the size it does in different situations can be improved by some simple tests.

First, consider the Moon as viewed well up in the sky. The most famous experiment about the Moon's size is holding a dime out at arm's length and finding that the dime easily hides the Moon. Try it! You will learn that a dime is much too big—so find the smallest paper disk that suffices.

The Moon can almost fit within the bowl of the tiny dipper formed by the brightest stars of the Pleiades cluster. Compare them yourself when both Moon and Pleiades are up. The Moon could be wedged between apex and base of the minute Lambda Orionis triangle of stars in Orion's head. Compare Moon and triangle with both up and the Moon not bright.

Next, turn your attention to what physicist Jearl Walker has called "probably the most striking illusion in the natural landscape."

What may be the oldest known scientific theory for the "Moon Illusion" (at least as old as Ptolemy, who mentions it) is one that partly—but only partly—explains the effect. This is the idea that the low Moon can be compared, side by side, with distant earthly objects that we know are large yet appear small due to their distance. However, Minnaert claims that the low Moon still looks unusually large, even when viewed through a tube that cuts it off from the landscape. Try this.

Minnaert's excellent discussion in his classic *The Nature of Light and Color in the Open Air* argues that the Moon Illusion's cause is our perception of the shape of the sky—specifically, a number of factors that can lead to the sky seeming more distant than usual near the horizon. Your small coin will cover the seemingly hugest rising Moon quite as easily as it does a high Moon (in fact, a bit more easily because the Moon is a little closer to an observer when overhead than when near the horizon). Suppose, however, as Minnaert says, that twilight, cloudiness, or the presence of distant earthly objects all do make the sky near the horizon seem

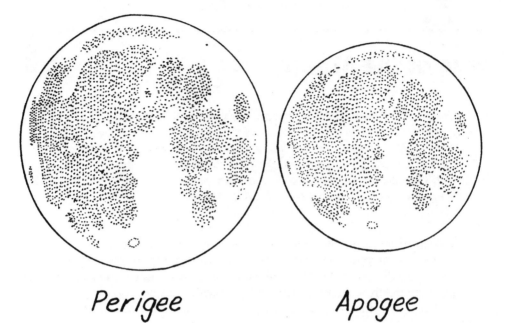

Perigee   Apogee

Apparent sizes of the Moon at perigee (closest) and apogee (farthest).

farther than usual. Wouldn't a same-size-as-always Moon in a more distant sky seem bigger?

These ideas need testing! How subjective are our impressions about the Moon's apparent size? Get several (or many) people to do the tests independently, and then compare the results. Have them answer question 2 below. Minnaert suggests a good way to get a numerical estimate of how much larger the low Moon looks than the high Moon: Impress on your mind how large the low Moon appears in front of you, then turn around (side-by-side comparison would destroy the illusion) to compare the impression with a series of white disks of different sizes on a dark background at a standard distance. Minnaert says such tests show a low Moon or Sun may sometimes look 2.5 to 3.5 times larger than a high one!

But there is a final supposed determinant of the shape of the sky, and thus, of the apparent size of the low Moon. Gauss proposed it, Minnaert supported it, and we should test it. Gauss claimed that the direction of our gaze in relation to our body affects our judgment of distances and sizes. Does, as Gauss and Minnaert maintain, the Moon look smaller whenever the gaze is directed upward (in relation to the body)? If they are correct, then leaning forward, so that you have to lift your gaze up to see the low Moon, will dispel the Moon Illusion, will make the Moon look its normal size. See if this works!

Questions

1. Can you find an object as common as a dime that more precisely covers the Moon when held at arm's length? What other asterisms or clusters besides the Orion and Pleiades ones are about the size of the Moon?

2. Is the Moon Illusion dispelled by looking through a tube that blocks view of distant comparison objects? How is the Moon Illusion affected by distant earthly objects, various kinds of cloudiness, twilight, and the direction of your gaze relative to your body?

8.

Brightness of the Moon's Disk and Moonlight

Discover at what lunar phases you have just enough moonlight to read print of various sizes by. Learn how far from a given streetlight you must be before your shadow, cast by that night's Moon, is as prominent as your shadow cast by the streetlight. Do detailed experiments to determine the faintest stars you can see at different distances in the sky from the Moon. Try to reproduce Sir John Herschel's famous comparison of the Moon's surface brightness to that of dark Earth rock.

The best print to use for the first part of this activity is a widely available standard size—for instance, that of a famous newspaper or magazine. Try to make sure that light other than the Moon's is not contributing significantly to the illumination of the print. Experiment to see how much the clearness of the night affects your results. Do not keep struggling to see a certain size print by the smallest lunar phase possible (you will strain your eyes!); accept the smallest phase at which you can read the print without strain.

A rather precise way to determine the brightness of a given night's Moon is to walk away from a particular streetlight until (1) you first detect your shadow cast by the Moon or (2) that shadow becomes as prominent as your shadow cast by the steetlight. Due to today's light pollution in many locales, you might find even the first of these results difficult to obtain with any but a nearly Full Moon.

Manmade light pollution certainly complicates the task of discovering what the naked-eye *limiting magnitude* (faintest magnitude visible) is for stars at different lunar phases and at different distances from the Moon in the sky. The angular altitude of the Moon in the sky (especially if the Moon is low) and *transparency* (clearness of atmosphere) of the particular night must also be taken into account. But none of these difficulties is insurmountable. And the knowledge of how well various sky objects can be observed under different moonlight and other sky conditions is invaluable. Such knowledge can gain you many sights you didn't think you could get, and it can save you from many frustrating late-night outings you didn't know would be fruitless.

Finally, you can demonstrate to yourself the distinction between the Moon's great total brightness and its quite meager *albedo* (reflectivity). The albedo of the Moon is only about .06. (The Moon only reflects about 6 percent of sunlight hitting it.) That is the albedo of quite dark rock. And that is precisely what Sir John Herschel noted when the rising Moon looked darker than Table Mountain, which the setting Sun was illuminating as his ship approached Cape Town, South Africa. Minnaert suggests recreating this experiment with a white wall to replace the mountain, but other objects could be used. Minnaert stresses that, for this observation to be completely accurate, the setting Sun and rising Moon should be at the same altitude (thus equally dimmed by Earth's atmosphere), which would happen around Full Moon (or a number of hours before the moment of Full, to be precise).

Questions

1. What is the smallest lunar phase by which you can read print of a particular standard size? How does different "transparency" (clearness) on various nights affect your results? What phases give straight-on moonlight equal to the illumination level of a horizontal plane at different stages of twilight? (See Activity 52.) What activities other than reading become possible at particular lunar phases?

2. How far must you be from a streetlight before the Moon at various phases will cast from you a discernible shadow? How far must you be before your Moon shadow is stronger than your shadow cast by the streetlight?

3. What is the magnitude of the faintest stars visible at different angular distances from the Moon at each phase, at different altitudes, and at different levels of sky transparency?

9.

Lunar Occultations and Conjunctions with Stars and Planets

Observe the faintest stars that can be seen with the naked eye when in close conjunctions with the Moon—for each lunar phase. Try to determine which is the least bright star or planet you can observe with the naked eye, right up to the edge of the Moon before the Moon occults it.

This activity is really a special extension of one part of the previous activity (the part addressed by question 3 of that activity). But here we are interested not just in judging the Moon's brightness or in knowing whether certain objects will be visible to the naked eye at a particular lunar phase, we are interested in whether certain examples of those marvelous events called *conjunctions* and *occultations* will be visible without optical aid.

A conjunction is, loosely speaking, any close meeting of two celestial objects (in its stricter definition, a conjunction occurs when one celestial object passes due north or south of another). An occultation is a conjunction so close that one of the objects actually does pass in front of the other.

Seeing a planet or star as an elusive glimmer extremely close to the Moon is a remarkable sight. Determine how close to the Moon you can see objects of various magnitudes at different lunar phases. (As usual, the objects' altitudes, the presence of city light pollution, and the sky transparency all will be complicating factors.)

You may notice that the Moon is, night by night or hour by hour, getting closer to certain objects with which you become fairly sure it will have close conjunction. But you are going to have to read some astronomical magazines or almanacs to know in advance when an actual occultation will occur. If you cannot spend any money, then you can go to your local library. One good source of occultation information is David Dunham's articles in each January issue of *Sky & Telescope*.

The naked-eye challenge at an occultation is to see the object without optical aid when the object is virtually right on the Moon's edge. Needless to say, this will be far easier if it is the unlit edge of the Moon and the lunar phase is small. How faint can stars be and be seen in this way under the best conditions? Dunham recently pointed out a few instances of possible naked-eye visibility of third-magnitude stars at the Moon's very edge in two *grazing occultations* (occultation in which the star blinks on and off as it goes behind peaks and highlands on Moon's edge)!

Questions

1. What are the faintest objects you can see in close (how close?) conjunction with the Moon at different phases? How is this affected by city lights, weather, and the objects' altitude?

2. What are the faintest objects you can see right on the Moon's edge at start or end of an occultation? In such cases, are you still helped by averted vision? (See Activity 27.)

10.

Color of the Moon's Disk

Record, at each day's end, when the Moon first turns yellow and when it appears yellowest— noting the effects of sky transparency, clouds, and twilight glow on the timing and degree of yellowness. Make careful notes of sky conditions when you see Moons of unusual color. Compare the Moon's typical color with that of the brightest planets.

What is the color of the Moon as seen from Earth? Since the lunar landscape is mostly a neutral gray, the Moon should show us the same color as the sunlight that illuminates it. (Actually sunlight loses a little bit of the bluer wavelengths in being reflected from the Moon, so moonlight is marginally redder.) Both Sun and Moon do shine basically yellow-white—more white than yellow, though, due to the addition of the light of blue sky and the fact that any light vastly brighter than its background tends to be perceived as white by the eye. But in different situations, the Moon takes on a variety of other colors that need to be better understood and can be better understood through this activity.

The Moon might, of course, become a deeper gold or honey color when low on a hazy night or even orange or reddish when low in a very hazy sky. But more interesting is the pure white to pure yellow to yellowish white change the Moon typically makes from day to twilight to night in a clear sky. The Moon of day is china white due to so much light of the blue sky (scattered sunlight from air molecules) combining with its natural yellow-white. In a night sky the Moon seems yellow-white, but with only weak yellow because, in this case, the dominance of white must be largely due to the Moon being vastly brighter than its background. But what happens in between? At some point near or during twilight, the Moon often takes on, rather briefly, a seemingly pure yellow. Obviously this is in part because the blue skylight scattered by the Sun has faded; but part may be (as M. Minnaert suggests) because of the color contrast with the still faintly blue background. To test these ideas (and also to enjoy the colors), record exactly when you first see and when you most see yellow in the Moon at the end of many different days. Note the Moon's phase and altitude and the sky conditions. (Compare especially the surrounding sky's color and brightness with the Moon's.)

There are special colors that the Moon may appear to have around twilight, due to the Moon's contrast with the colors of clouds and twilight glows when they are present. The near Full Moon becomes bronze yellow when we see it in the midst of the blue-gray earthshadow. (See Activity 51.) The crescent Moon may look distinctly green when seen near purple-red clouds after sunset, or especially when it is surrounded by volcanically enhanced purple light twilight glow. (See Activity 53.) In fact, the counter purple light (see Activity 55) in the east at dusk was so strong on some occasions after 1982's El Chichón eruption, that I saw astonishingly green Full Moons a few times. Such an effect should not be confused with the famous "blue moon" (or green moon or blue sun or green sun), which, on very rare occasions, is caused by scattering by particles of the correct size in the pall from certain forest fires and volcanic eruptions. Keep a look out for all such unusual Moon colors (including at Moon eclipses), and make careful notes about their circumstances. (By the way, perhaps the rarest colored moon was the purple moon seen from New England in 1950 when a red total eclipse combined with a blue moon!)

Compare the Moon's color with that of the bright planets Venus and Jupiter. Can you decide which is yellower? Try looking at a "star" of the Moon through a tiny pinhole in cardboard to see if this aids comparison.

Questions

1. When does the Moon start turning pure yellow, and when is it yellowest, at day's end? How do the purity of yellow and the timing of these events depend on the Moon's phase, altitude, position relative to twilight glows, and the sky's clearness? Does time of maximum yellowness correspond with time of maximum (naked-eye) visibility of lunar features? (See Activity 1.)

2. What are the circumstances of your observations of red, orange, pink, bronze-yellow, blue, black, green, or purple moons?

3. Is the Moon more or less yellow than Venus and Jupiter?

11.

Color of Moon Shadows and Moonlit Landscape and Sky

Try to perceive the color of a moonlit landscape and estimate what hue it is.
Also estimate at what phase such color becomes visible and to what extent it is
the color of the objects themselves. Then, try to perceive the color of Moon
shadows by comparing them with the shadows produced by various kinds of
streetlights.

What is the color of a landscape illuminated by moonlight? When the Moon is bright enough, some of this color may be that of the objects in the landscape themselves. But the color of a moonlit landscape is often regarded (and rendered by painters) as blue-white, silver-white, or blue-green. Why should a landscape lit by the Moon, an object very slightly redder than the Sun (see beginning of Activity 10), seem bluer than a daytime landscape?

One reason is that the human eye is relatively more sensitive to the blue end of the spectrum at low light levels, so blue (or the blue component of) light sources are seen relatively brighter. (This is called the *Purkinje effect*.)

The other reason is that moonlight is scattered from the blue sky. (This blue light must, therefore, be especially prominent in Moon shadows, which are blocked from direct moonlight.) Determine at what lunar phase you can first see a hint of blue in the night sky. Look for objects' own color, and decide at what phase such colors first become visible.

These observations may have to be carried out as much as possible away from the direct influence of artificial lights. But streetlights—at least in limited number and intensity—can help make the color of Moon shadows more noticeable. Compare the color of your shadow cast by moonlight with your shadow cast by a streetlight. See how the visibility and apparent hue of Moon shadows (affected by contrast with the color of the streetlight-illuminated ground) differ when compared with shadows made by incandescent, mercury vapor, and other lights.

Questions

1. What is the color of a moonlit landscape? At what phase can you first detect some blue in the sky? Some color in objects themselves?
2. How does the color of Moon shadows compare with the color of shadows caused by various kinds of streetlights?

Moonlit landscape with Moon shadows.

12.

Thinnest Moons in Twilight and Day

Try to observe the crescent Moon the soonest before and after New Moon possible—both with the Sun below the horizon and with the Sun above the horizon.

The factor that usually defeats one's attempts to see a very thin Moon is bad weather—even light cloud or haze down low where the Moon will appear may hide a very slender crescent.

The astronomical factors are several. The angle of the ecliptic (well, actually the angle of the Moon's path) to the horizon must be as steep as possible so that the Moon's elongation (angular separation from the Sun) is as much in the vertical as possible. Such an angle occurs in the spring for the "young moon" (in the west just after sunset) and in the autumn for the "old moon" (in the east just before dawn)—as seen from mid-northern latitudes. Less important, but significant, is that the Moon be moving fast in its orbit around the time of the New Moon in question. When doing so, it achieves a greater elongation from the Sun in less time. The Moon moves fastest in its orbit and in our sky when it is closest to us at *perigee,* so one should have a perigee near New Moon for an ideal shot at a thin Moon. By the way, not just astronomy magazines but good almanacs do list the dates of perigees. (Ottewell's *Astronomical Calendar* each year has superb young and old moon finder charts.) And most almanacs do give the exact moments of New Moons, so you can easily compute the Moon's age (even though elongation from the Sun is really the criterion which determines how thin the Moon is).

Any Moon much less than about 30 hours from New Moon is notable. Records for the youngest Moon ever seen with the naked eye include a claim of 14½ hours by two English housemaids on the night of a zeppelin attack in World War I and a better documented case of 14 hours, 51 minutes from New Mexico on May 5, 1989. Earlier that same evening in 1989, Robert Victor set the record for optical aid by observing, with 11 by 80 binoculars, a young moon just 13 hours, 28 minutes after New Moon!

What is the thinnest sliver of illuminated Moon that can ever be seen? It can be calculated that, even when still quite a few degrees from the Sun, the Moon's last illuminated parts will be eaten up by the shadows of mountains at the edge of the Moon. But the exact elongation at which this happens (variable in any case because of libration) must be determined by observation. A. Danjon's studies suggested that the crescent becomes invisible when the Moon comes within 7 degrees of the Sun—which means at least for a while every month.

Obtaining information on when the Moon is first visible after New actually is of practical benefit to historians and to certain religions that still have lunar calendars. Of little practical importance but of great enjoyment is looking for the thinnest crescent you can see with the Sun still above the horizon. Once, purely by chance as I gazed up my state's tallest hickory tree in daytime, I spied a surprisingly young Moon high in the southwest. With planning and effort, a very much younger Moon could be observed in a blue sky.

What will an ultrathin Moon in twilight look like, and what should you note when you see it? You should record the exact time of your naked-eye (and binocular) sighting. You should note how much less than 180 degrees around the Moon's circumference the lit part extends. If the Moon is less than 24 hours from New you may see dark breaks in the crescent—note or draw the locations of these. A good sketch or photo of such a Moon would be wonderful.

Questions

1. What are the "youngest" and "oldest" moons you can spot? How do the following factors affect visibility of moons of certain ages: brightness of twilight (a function of the Sun's distance below the horizon, not just time after sunset or before sunrise); altitude of the Moon (including when last visible—2 degrees above the horizon? 3 degrees?); and transparency of the atmosphere.

2. How much less than a 180-degree semicircle is the crescent? If there are any breaks in the crescent, where are they? How poor (as measured by star-twinkling) must the "seeing" be for a moon of particular thinness to display naked-eye beads of light moving along it?

3. How thin (or young or old) a Moon can you see in the day?

13.

Earthshine on the Moon

Observe "earthshine" on the night part of the Moon, estimating its intensity at each phase month after month. Try to correlate your observations with cloudiness or clearness on TV weather satellite photos of the part of the Earth then shining on the Moon.

Everyone has noticed at times the dark part of the Moon shining softly beside the brighter sunlit crescent. This is earthshine, for it is actually the light of our own planet illuminating part of the Moon's night side.

What is most interesting about earthshine is that its intensity varies, and not just with the Moon's phase. Earthshine generally becomes harder to see as the crescent gets thicker and brighter because (1) the crescent's light overwhelms the dim earthshine more and more, and (2) Earth, as seen from the Moon, is then itself showing an ever-smaller phase. (The Earth's phase seen from the Moon is always the complement of the Moon's phase seen from Earth.) But why does earthshine vary even at the same phase from one month to the next? The answer is that the sunlit part of Earth shining on the Moon sometimes has more or less land or ocean or more or less cloudiness on it. Clouds are highly reflective, and a cloudy face of sunlit Earth makes the strongest earthshine. Nowadays it is possible for many of us to see TV weather that shows satellite photos of much of the Earth—opening the possibility of easily correlating our earthshine observations with weather conditions thousands of miles away. Try it!

But how does one go about accurately rating the intensity of earthshine? Try a 0 to 10 rating system, which, fortunately, can be made more accurate by certain key points of visibility. Your lowest rating is, of course, if earthshine is altogether invisible. On the other hand, the visibility of the maria by earthshine becomes

Earthshine on the Moon.

possible when earthshine is very strong. How many features you detect gives you further criteria.

Notice just how brightness of twilight, sky transparency, and the Moon's altitude all affect earthshine. Find out the soonest time after sunset (or before sunrise) that earthshine can be seen. Does haziness conceal earthshine easily? Even on a clear night, there should be an altitude at which anything but very strong earthshine disappears as the Moon drops lower and shines through an ever longer pathway of air. This suggests a further criterion for judging the intensity of earthshine (at least when it is not extremely bright): Determine carefully what are the faintest stars visible at the altitude where earthshine disappears. (By the way, city light pollution would complicate these observations—even make earthshine harder to see.)

Questions

1. What is your rating of earthshine's intensity each night? What is your rating of the largest lunar phase at which you can still detect earthshine (with the naked eye)? What is the most lunar surface detail you can see by it? What is the soonest after sunset you can ever see it? How is it affected by sky transparency, brightness of twilight, and Moon's altitude?

2. Does great cloudiness on the part of the Earth shining on the Moon (most of Earth's daylit side when the Moon is a thin crescent) occur whenever you see strong earthshine?

14.

Judging Full Moons and Half Moons

Determine as closely as possible, by naked-eye observation alone, the exact times of Full Moon and First (or Last) Quarter. Also try to determine how far from the anti-solar point (in degrees) the Moon must be before some shading of its edge is evident to the naked eye.

The exact moments of Full Moon and half Moon (the Moon is half-lit at First and Last Quarter) can be seen every month from one hemisphere of Earth. You have only to check an almanac for the exact times: If the Moon is above the horizon where you are at these precise moments, you will see these phases.

But how close can the unaided eye, without the observer knowing the times in advance, come to determining the exact times of Full Moon and half Moon?

The answers are very different for Full and half moons. The time of half moon can be judged to within hours by the naked eye; the time of Full Moon can sometimes not be judged to within a day or two.

Part of the reason for the difference is the fact that, at First (or Last) Quarter, the apparent movement of the terminator (line separating light and dark) is greatest. (This is simply a matter of perspective, resulting from foreshortening of the lunar landscape at the Moon's left and right edges, the parts traversed by the terminator near Full Moon).

But a big part of the reason is the human eye's inborn talent for recognizing straight lines precisely. When the Moon is half-lit, the terminator is most nearly a straight line. Variations in elevation on the Moon keep this line from being quite perfectly straight, of course. But the fact remains that the eye sees easily that the terminator is curved to the right the night before First Quarter and curved to the left the night after (as viewed from Earth's northern hemisphere). Learn how few hours before First Quarter you still see a slight curve to the terminator and how few hours after First Quarter you again see a curve to it. Do not bias yourself by knowing the precise time of the phase beforehand.

The goal of judging when Full Moon occurs, by looking for shading or noncircularity, is complicated in an interesting way by the Moon's orbit. Technically speaking, "Full Moon" occurs when the Moon is 180 degrees away from the Sun as measured in *ecliptic longitude*. But this does not mean the Full Moon always is at the *anti-solar point*, the point on the celestial sphere of the heavens exactly opposite the Sun. The Moon's orbit is tilted with respect to the plane of Earth's orbit, and so usually passes north or south of the anti-solar point at Full Moon—indeed even north or south of the Earth's shadow. (Were it not so, we would witness a lunar eclipse at every Full Moon.) So the Full Moon is rarely 100 percent lit—but is the slight shading left at a Full Moon ever large enough to detect without optical aid? Answer this question yourself by observations.

Questions

1. How near to the time of half moon can you still see a slight overall curve to the terminator? Is it more difficult in some months due to different features at the terminator because of libration?

2. How near to the time of Full Moon can you detect shading or non-circularity each month? If there are months when you can still see a shaded edge even at the moment of "Full Moon," how close in degrees must the Moon be to the anti-solar point (check a star map) before the shading cannot be detected?

PLANETS

15.

Differences Between Planets and Stars: Twinkling

Point out a star and planet of roughly similar brightness and altitude to people who do not know which is which, and see how many can guess correctly on the basis of which twinkles more. Tell the difference between a planet and a star by closing one eye and trying to eclipse each with overhanging branches or electric lines. Look at Mercury always, Mars and Venus when small or thin, or any planet when low, to see how strongly they twinkle.

How do we tell a planet from a star with the naked eye? Before long, a devoted amateur astronomer learns to keep track of where all the planets are, so there could rarely be confusion. But observing the visible differences between planets and stars, obviously helpful to a novice, also can bring a new dimension of direct appreciation to the more experienced observer.

A famous distinction between planets and stars is that stars twinkle and planets don't. Is this always true? Show a star and planet of about the same brightness and altitude to a group of people who do not know which is which, and see whether all of them can choose correctly which twinkles less and must therefore be a planet. Afterwards, you can get the people to look at each object with one eye closed and try blocking each object from view with a high or thin tree branch or electric wire: If the branch or wire subtends a very small angular arc, people will see that it can hide the star's light but not the planet's light completely. The reason, of course, is that planets, being so vastly closer, have quite sizable apparent disks whereas stars do not. And having light rays coming to us from all over a sizable disk guarantees that the image as a whole will not waver—twinkle— when some of the rays are diverted by atmospheric turbulence.

But can some planets' disks ever be small enough or the atmosphere unsteady enough for them to show pronounced twinkling? Observe to find out. Mercury appears small, is sometimes a crescent, and is seen with the naked eye low in the sky, where there is a greater total amount of turbulence and greater twinkling—always check it for twinkling. Venus, for quite a while before and after superior conjunction, can appear as small as Mercury. Then, when almost closest to Earth around inferior conjunction, its globe appears six times larger . . . but has only a very thin crescent of the earthward side of its globe lit! Mars can be high in a fully dark sky when its disk is less than half the size of Mercury's. Is this small enough to make Mars twinkle? If you see dependably large Saturn or dependably huge Jupiter twinkle strongly, the atmosphere must be terribly unsteady indeed.

Whatever pronounced twinkling you do see from planets could be equated with the level of star-twinkling seen in stars much higher in the sky—how high?

Questions

1. What percentage of people can distinguish a planet from a star (of similar brightness and altitude) by twinkling alone?

2. How easy is it to tell a planet and star apart by only the latter being eclipsible when you close one eye and try to block them from view with a high overhanging branch or wire? Is it much more difficult if the planet has a small apparent disk at the time?

3. How much twinkling do planets show when they are very low in the sky, or when the atmosphere is very unsteady, or when their disks are very small or very thin? Can you measure the twinkling of a low planet by finding at what higher altitude a star twinkles as much?

16.

Differences Between Planets and Stars: Planetary Motions

Determine the shortest time and the longest time it takes before you can notice a planet's change of position in relation to background stars.

In a moment or two, lack of twinkling may distinguish a planet from a star. But the very word *planet* is derived from the Greek for "wanderer" because the planets change their positions in relation to the fixed patterns of stars. How many nights—or mere hours—must you wait before a change in a planet's position is detected? As a benefit of doing this activity, you will learn more (and enjoy more) about the planets' movements than many a veteran planet watcher does!

With Mercury and Venus, the planets that can move with greatest apparent motion, there is often a problem of no background stars bright enough to be seen near them in the twilight sky they often inhabit. Mars can sometimes rival the fastest Venus and is then easily visible in a dark sky. Jupiter and Saturn are far slower but, like Mars, fastest when easily visible. All planets are slowest around the time when they reach their *stationary points*—events that are listed in good almanacs, though you may find them given as "——— begins retrograde motion," or "———halts retrograde motion."

Figures 3 and 4 show why and when inner and outer planets appear to halt

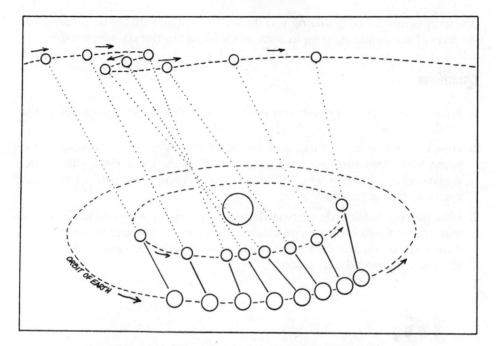

Figure 3 Explanation of retrograde motion of inferior planets.

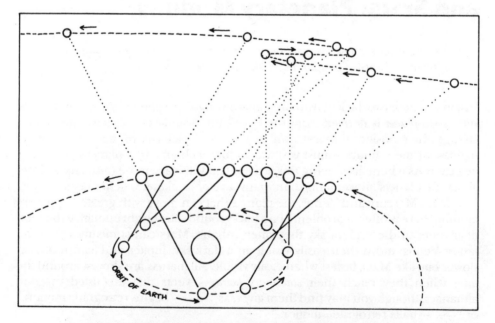

Figure 4 Explanation of retrograde motion of superior planets.

and retrograde—a motion that so puzzled astronomers before Copernicus that a complex system of *epicycles* had to be devised to explain it all (until the Copernican system showed an elegantly more simple—and correct—way to explain it). Note the further complication that, because the orbits of the planets are not quite in the same plane as Earth's, the path traced out during retrograde motion is usually a loop.

Studying such diagrams gives you the theoretical background to understand what happens. But to see the theory realized and get a feel for how it works in the different case of each planet, you must observe.

You will find it easiest to notice a planet's change in position if it is passing near a particular star or across an imaginary line between two stars. (Two appropriate stars can usually be found.)

Questions

1. What are the shortest and longest times it takes for you to detect each planet's motion in relation to the fixed background stars?

2. What is the order of apparent speeds of the planets at a certain time? How many planets are retrograding? Can you, from your own observations, chart the retrograde loops of several planets on a star map and compare their sizes and shapes? (The nearer they are to the projected plane of Earth's orbit, the line of the ecliptic, the flatter the loops.)

17.

Beginnings and Ends of Planetary Apparitions

See how near to the time of its conjunction with the Sun you can observe each planet—both low in the west at dusk before conjunction and low in the east at dawn after conjunction.

The term *apparition* is applied to the period of weeks or months during which a planet is visible between its successive spells of unviewability caused by its being near conjunction (close meeting) with the Sun in the sky. Planets farther from the Sun than Earth can only be in conjunction with the Sun when on the far side from us; planets nearer to the Sun than Earth can be at *superior conjunction* on far side or *inferior conjunction* on near side.

The object of this activity is to see as much of each apparition of a planet as possible with the naked eye. Besides being an enjoyable test of our abilities, this activity gets us out to see certain special sights that can only be seen near the start or the end of apparitions.

A few weeks before inferior conjunction, the brightness of Venus drops rapidly, but its crescent grows ever longer and thinner, so that its shape might just be glimpsed with the naked eye (see Activity 21) and strong twinkling might be noticed (see Activity 15). At a few apparitions in Venus' eight-year cycle of them, Venus can set a number of minutes after the Sun even on the day of inferior conjunction—and for a few days thereafter. This means it can be viewed as both Morning Star (before sunrise) and Evening Star (after sunset) on the same day. The next excellent chance for this rare sighting in the Northern Hemisphere is around April 1, 1993 and for the Southern Hemisphere around August 22, 1991. Another challenge is to see Venus (whether at dawn or dusk) on every day through inferior conjunction. (No other planet can be watched through conjunction; nor apparently can the Moon—see Activity 12.)

Then there is Mercury. Due to its inveterate closeness to the Sun in our sky, many observers only look for it near the peak of its best apparitions and consequently miss most of the drama of Mercury's behavior. For instance, unlike Venus, Mercury is brightest not long after superior conjunction. Glimpse Mercury soon after then, and you may see it when its magnitude will still exceed that of Sirius or even Jupiter! Of course, Mercury will be low in a twilight sky at the time and would *appear* less bright than Sirius does in a dark sky; but you could compare it with other stars (that are in much darker sky) to see how bright it does appear. You could study, during Mercury's apparitions, how its visibility varies as a function of

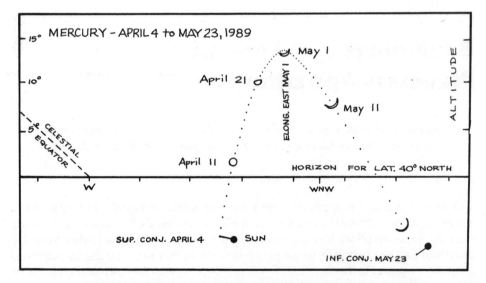

An apparition of Mercury (showing phases visible in telescopes only).

both its altitude *and* its brightness in the sky at various stages of twilight. (Of course, the variability of sky conditions would be a complicating factor.)

Think of the benefits of developing the ability to see a planet low in twilight. You would know in advance if you had a shot at that close but low twilight conjunction of two planets or at some other special sight.

What do you need to succeed in this activity? Admittedly, a pair of binoculars is a great assistance. (Even if you have them, always try seeing the planet with the naked eye after you find it with your optical aid.) Seeing a planet low in twilight may take a good knowledge of where to look for it (Astronomy magazines can often help with their charts.) But the most important requirements are simple: desire and perseverance.

Questions

1. How soon before and after conjunction with the Sun can you see each planet? How do your answers vary according to the season? How does the planet's altitude at stages of twilight affect your success, and at what altitude is the planet first, last, and best seen that day? Precisely how do sky conditions affect your figures?

2. What is the brightest magnitude at which Mercury can be glimpsed? How does its visibility vary as a function of both altitude at different stages of twilight and magnitude? How many days can you see Mercury (and each of the other planets) at an apparition? Can you see Mercury at every one of its apparitions in a year? Can you see Venus every day through inferior conjunction? As Morning and Evening Star the same day?

18.

Daytime and Bright Twilight Visibility of Venus

With the naked eye, observe Venus in the daytime as often as possible and as near to midday as possible. Find out how early in evening twilight or how late in morning twilight you can see it when sky conditions are not so good or when it is close to the Sun.

Venus is the only planet that can be rather easily seen with the unaided eye in the middle of the day. Of course, it helps to have a clear, deep blue sky and to have the planet both far from the Sun and especially bright. The major questions to explore in this activity are just how these factors—sky conditions and brightness and angular distance of Venus from the Sun—do affect daytime observations of the planet.

First, however, let us consider pointers and pitfalls concerning this kind of observation. The initial problem is knowing fairly accurately where to look. If you know Venus's current elongation from the Sun and whether it is now farther north or farther south on the Zodiac than the Sun, then you should be able to take into account the time of day and to narrow down the search area. (Which body is closer to its high point on the meridian, Sun or Venus?) Even so, binoculars are a help in the initial locating.

Another problem in daylight is your eyes falling into focus on some nearby tree or building rather than on infinity. A passing cloud or two may help you get that long focus you need. By the way, averted vision (see Activity 27) does not help in daytime lighting. (Venus is bright enough—as bright as at night—anyway.)

Do not get disappointed if you have difficulty at first. And if you decide to give up because the sky is hazy or because Venus is near the Sun (always block off that blinding Sun properly from your view!!), then try looking later in the day or as early in twilight as possible. Of course, a first convenient way to see the marvel of Venus in the same sky as the Sun it orbits is to follow the planet as the Sun rises. (Try using a branch, an electric line, or, especially, the Moon if it is nearby, to help you keep track of Venus's position).

Questions

1. Under what conditions can Venus be observed in the daytime with the naked eye? How much haze can be present, how dim can Venus be, and how close to the Sun in the sky can Venus be—for it to be seen in midday and before it can no longer be seen anytime during the day?

2. How early in dusk or late in dawn can Venus be seen with the naked eye at various elongations (angular distances) from the Sun? When sky conditions are not good?

19.

Daytime and Bright Twilight Visibility of Other Planets

With the naked eye, observe planets other than brilliant Venus as late in dawn or as early in dusk as possible. Find out how long after sunrise or before sunset you can see Jupiter, Mars, or even Saturn, when they are near their brightest.

See planets other than Venus in the daytime with the naked eye? You do not read about this being possible in many astronomy books, but it certainly is. On the morning of September 7, 1988, I took advantage of a rare opportunity and saw three planets—Venus, Jupiter, and Mars—at once with unaided vision up to 18 minutes after sunrise. (I had to drive off on an errand, or else I could have followed them longer). Of course, all three planets were quite well placed and brighter than magnitude −2 that morning. But a number of dedicated observers have seen objects of magnitude 0 just after sunrise and just before sunset.

The sightings extend from nineteenth century observers up to the present. These observers may have had especially keen vision for such sightings, or skill and enthusiasm may have played a greater role in at least some cases. But even if special vision was absolutely necessary for seeing magnitude 0 objects with the naked eye and with the Sun just above the horizon, that still would suggest that most people could view Jupiter fairly often and Mars occasionally (when as bright as magnitude −1 or −2) under similar conditions. I know two people who have both easily observed Jupiter (when it happened to be conveniently near the Moon) many hours after sunrise.

The presence of the Moon as a guide for keeping track of the planet's location in all that blue sky is very helpful. In addition, the tips provided in the previous activity hold true for this one, too; but here, truly at the limits of human vision, they become crucial. A deep blue sky, the planet high up and far from the Sun in the sky, a proper focus, a branch or wire as guide, a good knowledge of where to search, and the use of binoculars to locate—the more of these you have, the better.

Of course, you can be satisfied with achieving your personal best in this activity. Indeed, when Saturn and Mars are considerably dimmer than magnitude 0, or when sky conditions are not ideal, or when a planet's altitude or elongation from the Sun are not favorable, then there is no question of anyone seeing a planet with the naked eye when the Sun is above the horizon. The question is, at how bright a stage of twilight can you see it? And this is virtually as exciting—almost unexplored territory.

Questions

1. How long after sunrise or before sunset—or at least how near to these times in bright twilight—can you see planets with the naked eye?

2. How far into twilight can you see, with the naked eye, a planet in various conditions of sky transparency and various degrees of brightness, altitude, and elongation from the Sun?

20.

Trying to See the Moons of Jupiter with the Naked Eye

With the naked eye, attempt to glimpse a moon or two of Jupiter. Note time, date, and sky conditions. If possible, enlist other people at the time to determine whether they can independently see what you are seeing.

If someone did thorough research and gathered all published reports of naked-eye sightings of Jupiter's moons, I suspect the list would be fairly long. And yet this feat remains extremely rare, almost legendary. Does it require very sharp or otherwise exceptional vision? Having achieved it myself twice and not having tried it all that many times, I am pretty much convinced it does not demand excellent eyesight.

In one of my sightings, I noticed the moon that is the farthest out from Jupiter, of the large, Galilean satellites—Callisto. Another time, I saw the closer-to-Jupiter but brighter Ganymede. The latter was easier to see and continuously visible when I concentrated.

I attribute these successful observations to several factors. Although Jupiter was not at its closest to Earth, its highest of the night, or its highest in the zodiac, it was indeed rather favorably placed. I also felt that both nights were a little bit hazy, so that the "rays" of Jupiter seemed a bit diminished.

Whether a little haze really helps is arguable, but it does underline the fact that having the darkest, clearest sky is not essential; the four Galilean satellites are fifth-magnitude objects much of the time, even fourth magnitude occasionally. Nor, by itself, is the separation of Ganymede and Callisto from Jupiter the problem. As Figure 5 shows, even Io and Europa's maximum separation might be seen by very sharp-eyed observers, were it not for the fact that Jupiter is so bright. In practice, the impact of the hundreds of times brighter planet usually overwhelms

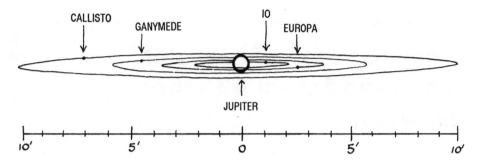

Figure 5 Apparent separations (in minutes of arc) of Galilean satellites from Jupiter (at an average opposition).

the impulse from Ganymede and Callisto on the eye. I regard as a bit dubious a few claims of children seeing all four Galilean moons at once!

Groups of people observing together might clarify to what extent differences in vision are important in these observations. It is probably best not to bias yourself by knowing beforehand where the moons are on a given night. But when you feel confident that you are seeing a point of light beside the planet, follow up your observation by using binoculars and/or checking the moons' positions in an astronomy magazine or an astronomy almanac. When you check for the moons, you should also make sure you are not just seeing a background star that happens to be near Jupiter at the time. (When such stars are near Jupiter, find out how far from it and how bright they are. They may prove a good introductory exercise to the more difficult task of a moon sighting.)

Questions

1. How many nights will you try before seeing a moon of Jupiter with the naked eye? If—or when—you do succeed, what conditions of the atmosphere and the planet's position and brightness do you feel permitted the success?

2. If you succeed in seeing a moon of Jupiter, how many of the people looking for it with you also succeed at that time?

21.

Trying to See the Shapes of Venus and Saturn with the Naked Eye

When conditions are optimum, attempt to see with the naked eye at least some indication of the crescent of Venus and the rings of Saturn.

Unlike seeing moons of Jupiter with the naked eye, detecting the shapes of the crescent Venus and, especially, of Saturn's rings may require unusually acute eyesight. The only time the Venus crescent extends for as much as about 1 arc-minute across is when it is getting rather close to the Sun in our sky. Saturn's ring system is never even that wide. But there is a distinction to be made: It should be easier to see the Venus or Saturn image a bit elongated than to make out actual crescent or rings.

I am not certain there is any strong evidence of the Venus crescent itself being seen with the naked eye. *Sky & Telescope's* Steve O'Meara, a man of notoriously gifted observing ability and eyesight, has told me of taking his fellow staffers out to see the crescent—and meeting with success. But it is unclear to me who of those people, if any, saw the actual crescent as opposed to some hint of shape of a slightly elongated form. (Would not sighting the actual shape have warranted an article or report in the magazine?) Of course, there are a number of individuals whose eyesight is as good as 20/10. If normal vision can see some shape, why haven't *they* seen and reported the crescent itself?

I suspect the problem is ignorance of when and how to try the observation. When Venus is a thin (but "giant") crescent, it is not far from inferior conjunction and therefore is low in the sky even right after sunset or right before sunrise. That is unfortunate because images low in the sky are poorer than high ones. The solution is to try viewing the planet well before sunset or well after sunrise, when it is higher and when the also treacherous problem of being distracted by long rays of Venus is reduced. (In bright light, the pupil is contracted so that we do not use the peripheral part of the lens whose distortions apparently are the principal cause of the rays.)

If you try our earlier Activity 18, you will gain experience in finding Venus in the daytime. If you decide that finding Venus at sunset is good enough, consider trying to see the crescent when it is slightly smaller but at a larger apparent separation from the Sun and thus higher. You might also consider trying only at the apparitions when Venus is quite steeply above the Sun just before or (in the morning) after inferior conjunction. But that means waiting a long time.

Even if you look for Venus as a huge crescent when it is favorably high in the day sky, you will only get your opportunity for a few weeks every 1½ years! On the other hand, trying to see the shape of Saturn with the naked eye can be attempted for several months each year—several months around the time Saturn is closest, in opposition to the Sun.

Through the early 1990s, Saturn will be having summer oppositions unfortunately low in the south for observers at midnorthern latitudes. You would be better off, however, trying in those years than in 1995 to 1996, the period when the rings are near edgewise and appear very thin. I can suggest one trick that might help a naked-eye observer see that Saturn's rings cause it to have an elongated shape. Minnaert mentions the experiment of looking at bright planets and stars through a 1-millimeter-wide pinhole centered in front of the eye in order to reduce rays. This is quite tricky to do, but it might be an aid in attempts to see Saturn's or Venus's shape in a dark or twilight sky. Needless to say, you should also pick for any of these observations a time when the atmosphere is steady as possible, with even most stars hardly twinkling.

Questions

1. Can you detect with the naked eye either the actual crescent of Venus or at least a slight elongation of its shape in the correct direction? Even if you cannot, under what conditions do you come closest; when is Venus a small, steady image? How near is Venus to inferior conjunction? How high is Venus in the sky? How important is having the "rays" short?

2. Can you detect a slight elongation of Saturn's image in the direction of the rings? Does looking through a 1-millimeter-wide eye-centered pinhole at Saturn help by reducing the rays? Is using the pinhole too difficult, or is Saturn too faint through it?

22.

Shadows Cast by the Brightest Planets

Attempt to see shadows cast by the brightest planets.

Another observing "feat" sometimes mentioned in books but perhaps rarely tried is looking for shadows cast by the planet Venus. There is no denying that, these days, it is not nearly so difficult to have Venus fairly high after twilight as it is to get a sky free enough of artificial lighting. But when you are at a country site, and Venus

Venus casting a shadow.

or Jupiter (which is fainter but more often high in a night sky) happens to be beaming brightly, be ready to try for this activity's marvelous result.

First, let us consider the conditions needed to see your shadow cast by planet-light. While it is obvious that there should be little if any skyglow from a city in the direction of Venus, it might not be so obvious that you might have to check a map to ensure this. Before a large section of sky turns livid with light pollution, there is a loss of its darkness that is not always recognized by the casual observer. Check your map and the limiting magnitudes of stars in that part of the sky,

Next, you need a very light-colored surface (sand, or a sheet you bring along), and you must make certain this surface, or "screen," is lit by as little light as possible from other sources—artificial or natural. You may have another area of sky brightened by city skyglow or even by the natural glow from Earth's atmosphere (airglow) and from the stellar multitudes helping to illuminate the subtle shadows you are hoping to see. The solution is finding ground open only to a small section of sky containing Venus—as you could in a forest.

Assuming these strict conditions (a big assumption!), you should clearly be able to see your shadow cast by Venus. In fact, Richard Keen (*Sky & Telescope*, December 1975, p. 382) reported sighting shadows cast by Jupiter when it was at magnitude -2.4 and calculated that shadows cast by an overhead object as dim as magnitude -1.0 (thus Sirius at -1.4) overhead might just be visible. Derek Wallentine later (*Sky & Telescope*, March 1977. p. 174) saw shadows from Jupiter at magnitude -2.3 and suggested that one-quarter-inch tall print might then have been readable in its light!

Despite Keen's calculation, I wonder if considerably fainter stars might produce shadows under extraordinary conditions. I think of a description I have read of magnitude 0 Vega rising like a lantern over Australia's Ayers Rock, where observers reported seeing their shadows cast by the Milky Way. Closer to home— perhaps *in* your home if you live far out in the country—there is Minnaert's experiment to let the light of a bright planet or star into a dark room to see *shadow bands*. (See Activity 93). The possibility of such an observation reaffirms to me that it may even be possible to see shadows of objects cast by the brighter stars out in nature.

Questions

1. Can you see your shadow cast by Venus or even by Jupiter? What does the shadow look like (sharp, prominent, wavering. . .)?

2. What pointers other than those suggested above are helpful in making the shadow visible, or more visible?

23.

Estimating the Brightness and Color of Planets

Try estimating the brightness of planets at different times by comparing them to stars of known, unvarying brightness. Rate the color of planets on a scale (also for stars) ranging from very blue to red.

How bright is Jupiter or Mars tonight? You can get an answer from an astronomy magazine or an astronomy almanac. But until the 1980s, the magnitudes given in these publications were up to one-third, even one-half a magnitude off for some of the planets! The new formulas for predicting the magnitudes seem much better. But the reflectivity of at least Jupiter and Mars is variable enough for the eye to detect their departures from predicted brightness sometimes. And what other reasons are there for checking the brightness of the planets yourself? Good fun and valuable observing exercise.

Estimating the brightness of Venus and Jupiter is tricky, because there are no other objects in their typical brightness range. Jupiter at brightest can almost equal Venus at faintest, and the latter's brightness is pretty well known. You can use it as a rough check on the former's brightness. Mercury scarcely escapes from twilight and is low, but is sometimes at similar altitude to good nearby comparison stars. Saturn and Mars almost always have good comparison stars available when high in the heavens, as they often are. In years when the angle of Saturn's rings changes markedly, it is fascinating to follow their effect on the brightness of the naked-eye point of light we call Saturn. Mars is even better. This planet's brightness changes over a range of three to five magnitudes in many years, much of the change occurring in a single season and in a fully dark sky. Jupiter's cloud activity can cause it to vary more from predicted brightness, but Mars's famous dust storms can sometimes make a brightness difference noticeable to the careful observer. Finally, the connoisseur of planet brightnesses will enjoy following the slight changes of distant fifth-magnitude Uranus from year to year.

Remember that all brightness estimates must allow for atmospheric extinction at different angular altitudes. (See Table 3 and Activity 32.)

Part 2 of this activity is planet colors, and it is no less fascinating than planet brightness. Here, as in the study of star colors, we attempt to learn not only about the actual colors of the objects but also about the physiology of the eye and the vocabulary of color. Here we also use a scale of colors like that given with Activity 25 (star colors). Indeed, study of the more numerous examples of hues presented by stars helps greatly in getting a feel for the use of the scale.

Always a problem in rating colors is the different brightnesses of objects.

Only when Venus and Jupiter are not greatly different in brightness can one compare their shades of yellow. But deeper gold Saturn is far dimmer. Could we use a small pair of binoculars on it to make its brightness seem comparable to the naked-eye Venus? Comparing the color of Saturn to many different first-magnitude stars is easy. A problem with Mercury is that haze down low often makes it look more orange than it is. Mars is the most noticeably colored of the planets and is very interesting to compare in hue with the red giant stars Betelgeuse and Antares when Mars is near them and similarly bright. The presence of dust storms can supposedly reduce Mars's ruddiness enough for the naked eye to note. Some people have better sensitivity to red than others, so compare your color estimates of Mars with those of other observers. (See Activity 25.)

Questions

1. What are the brightnesses of the planets tonight according to your estimates? How closely do these compare with the predicted values?

2. Can you make a case for Mars or Jupiter being a bit brighter or fainter than predicted at a certain time, due to atmospheric activity on these worlds?

3. What are the colors of the planets on the scale given in Activity 25? Is Mars ruddier than Betelgeuse or Antares when similarly bright? Is Mars less ruddy at times—for instance, during Martian dust storm activity?

24.

Special Aspects of Planetary Conjunctions

Use the opportunities of planetary conjunctions to more closely compare planet (and nearby star) colors, brightnesses, and "ray-spread" diameters.

The beauty of two planets poised near each other in the sky, two planets in "conjunction," is one of the greatest in astronomy. But looking more closely at these events can teach us not only the finer points of their loveliness; it can also teach us some properties of the planets (and surrounding stars) we did not know.

Our previous activity dealt with planet colors and brightnesses. Clearly, a conjunction (whether of two planets or of one planet with a star) is an especially good opportunity for comparing two objects' brightness and colors.

Planet in conjunction with the Moon.

There is, however, a remarkable limitation to the use of color comparison in conjunctions.

The limitation I speak of is the human mind-eye system's property of artificially enhancing a hue in proximity to its complementary color. Many telescopic *double stars* are famous for their startling contrasting hues—for instance, blue and gold or red and green—but each member of the pair's color is not as strong when viewed by itself.

A star like Regulus shows vivid blue when yellow Venus or red Mars is near it. This blue—and the planets' seemingly enhanced yellow and red—must be, in part, an artifact of this property of human vision. Of course, the fact it is an artifact makes it no less beautiful nor, perhaps, less revealing. Watch how the apparent colors of the objects seem to change as the distance between them changes. Your observations could give us a better measure of the objects' true colors as perceived by human vision (we already have instrumental measures) and of the hue-intensifying effect of complementary color proximity.

The apparent angular diameter of a star or planet's spread of "rays" is partly a function of how open the pupils of the observer's eyes are. (This depends in part on how dark the environment is and how long the eyes have had to adapt to that dark.) But of course the size of the ray-spread is largely a function of how bright the object is: A brighter planet has a wider ray-spread than a fainter one. Some naked-eye observers of the past and present have judged that even brilliant Venus and Jupiter may be no more than 2 to 3 arc-minutes in diameter of ray-spread to the average fully dark-adapted eye—no more than one-tenth the apparent diameter of the Moon. But what do you think? Conjunctions can be an opportunity to compare at least the relative sizes of ray-spreads. A conjunction must be extremely close before the ray-spreads of two planets start overlapping—or even merge—as seen with the naked eye. But a devoted observer should, with a little luck, be able to witness this breathtaking sight a few times in his or her life.

A conjunction is also a good opportunity to get a better feel for other angular sizes and distances. Test your judgment of angular distances by guessing how far apart the two objects are each night. Be amazed at how close a conjunction must be before the Moon could not fit between the pair and how splendid much more distant conjunctions than this appear.

Questions

1. How much effect does the decreasing distance between two planets (or between a star and a planet) have on two things: (1) the precise hues you rate them to be (on our color scale) and (2) the prominence with which those hues are visible?

2. Relatively how much wider in ray-spread is the brighter object than the fainter object in different conjunctions?

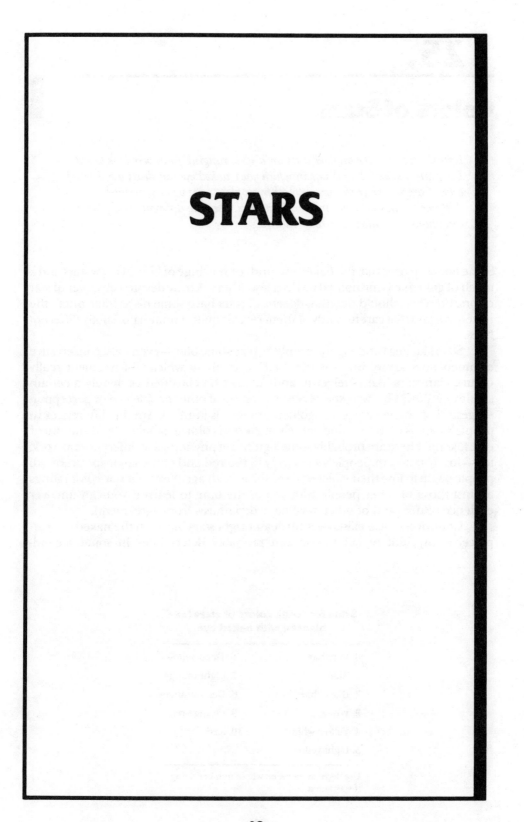

STARS

25.

Colors of Stars

Rate the colors of the brighter stars on a scale ranging from very blue to red. Determine the least bright star in which your naked eye can detect any hint of color. Compare your ratings with other people's to see what systematic differences exist and what may explain them. See how different atmospheric conditions may affect your color ratings.

Some books suggest that the naked eye finds only a tinge of blue in a few stars and a touch of gold that is misnamed red in a few others. A truly devoted observer of star colors, however, should find that dozens of stars have some discernible tint to the naked eye and that careful study of them reveals quite a number of subtly different hues.

Stars like Vega and Rigel certainly display some blue—even most conservative commentators agree. But it is the "red" stars about which disagreement really occurs. Can stars like Betelgeuse and Antares be classified as merely a certain shade of yellow? My own experience and testing of other people's color perception suggests that, at the very least, "golden orange" is justified. Are the differences in people's ratings of these colors merely matters of color vocabulary (and amount of care taken)? There are probably some significant physiological differences at work, too—for instance, in people's sensitivity to the red end of the color spectrum. All people begin to lose their violet-end sensitivity with age. Test your star-color ratings against those of other people with you at the time to learn if you can uncover evidence of this (and of other systematic departures from agreement).

Controversy also exists over the least bright stars in which the naked eye can perceive any hint of color. You can probably detect hues in some second-

---

Scale for rating colors of stars (and planets) with naked eye

0. Very blue	6. Deep yellow
1. Blue	7. Light orange
2. Blue-white	8. Deep orange
3. White	9. Orange-red
4. Yellow-white	10. Red
5. Light yellow	

Use decimals between whole number ratings if warranted.

magnitude stars. But are there any fainter ones that show color? Connected with this question is the effect of atmospheric conditions on star color. A lot of twinkling in stars foils attempts to rate their colors because part of that twinkling may be significant color changes caused by atmospheric turbulence. Investigate this matter and also whether different amounts of atmospheric transparency have important effects on the prominence of star colors.

Questions

1. On the accompanying 0 to 10 scale, what are the colors of the brightest stars? What is the least bright star in which you can detect a hint of color with the naked eye?

2. How do your color ratings of stars compare with those of other people? Do you notice any differences that are consistent with some people being more sensitive to the red end of the spectrum? Do older people tend to see less blue in the blue stars or to exhibit other differences from younger observers?

26.

Color Variations and Twinkling of Stars: "Seeing"

Measure the "seeing" at your observing site by rating, on a 0 to 10 scale, the amount of twinkling noticed in stars at various altitudes. Also notice at what altitude bright stars show no color changes. Keep a record of the seeing, and compare your results with the weather conditions, including the position of upper-air barometric highs and lows. Measure seeing from other places you visit, even those not far from your usual site if topography varies a lot in your area.

Seeing is the astronomer's term for the steadiness of images seen through our atmosphere. When the atmosphere is calm, the seeing is good: In telescopes, planetary detail is visible and close double stars can be split. For naked-eye observers, however, the chief indicator of the seeing is how much twinkling one observes in the stars.

The stars' twinkling, or *scintillation,* is a lovely thing to study more closely. But if you can learn to rate the seeing on the basis of star-twinkling, you will have the benefit of knowing what kind of telescopic views to expect on any given night and what size or kind of telescope it will be worth your while to take out. Don't own a telescope? Still, this activity can give you fascinating insights into how our atmosphere affects what we see of the stars.

Begin with our ever-useful 0 to 10 scale. Notice how many distinct twinkles or pulses of stars occur in 5 seconds, or 10—and not just of stars at one altitude, but also those at different altitudes, with each altitude bearing its own quality of seeing. (Generally, the higher you look—the less atmosphere gazed through—the better the seeing.) Perhaps there will be a certain altitude at which a most marked transition from little twinkling to much twinkling occurs. What is that altitude on different nights?

Since colors are wavelengths of light, and different wavelengths are bent in varying amounts by turbulence in our atmosphere, a star that twinkles a lot also begins to display color changes and darting rays of different colors. A careful naked-eye look reveals its presence in fairly bright stars (what is the dimmest?)—at least it does when they are low in the sky. Note the altitude at which color changes cease on various nights.

How near to the observer and how high up in the atmosphere are the conditions that determine the seeing? The answer depends upon the situation. Usually the turbulence higher up is what really matters. Steve Albers suggests that, when turbulence associated with more local convective weather is not involved (as it often is for much of North America in summer), a fairly straightforward guide to the seeing you can expect may be provided by the so-called upper-air highs and lows. These are sometimes mentioned on weather broadcasts (especially on detailed ones like those of cable TV's Weather Channel). Just as with *surface* highs and lows, it is where the circulations of these systems combine to increase winds and where their isobars run closest together that you can expect the highest winds, greatest changes in wind speed, and generally great turbulence. The high-altitude *jet streams* (often marked by the presence of certain clouds) generally should produce bad seeing.

Finally, the geography near you—mountains or large bodies of water—may have special effects on your seeing. Make observations to measure these seeing differences. Wherever you live, you can also study seeing differences in time— especially the rapid changes. (Sometimes these are identifiable even in a matter of minutes.)

Questions

1. How good or bad is tonight's seeing on a 0 to 10 scale judged according to the amount of star-twinkling? How many twinkles (and how many color changes) do stars at various altitudes in the sky undergo in a given short period of time? At what altitude is the transition from little twinkling to much twinkling? At what altitude is the transition from no or few color changes to many? What is the least bright star in which you can detect color changes?

2. Can you determine where most of the turbulence causing your bad seeing is coming from? Can you correlate the position of upper-air highs and lows and the jet stream with your seeing?

3. How is seeing affected by various notable topographical features (if such exist in your area)? What causes various instances of rapid changes in seeing at one location?

27.

Limiting Magnitude of Stars: Transparency

Attempt to determine your limiting magnitude on different moonless nights (and in different places) by seeing the faintest star possible with your naked eye—both high in the sky and low at various altitudes. Do the same with more extended (less pointlike) deep-sky objects. Compare your results with those of other people observing with you. Compare these nighttime measures of sky transparency with daytime measures. Note various weather statistics at the time of your observations, and see which weather patterns affect transparency. Compare the transparency and seeing, and find what kinds of weather patterns produce the best combination of the two.

I have stated that this activity is for moonless nights. (Activity 8 includes determining limiting magnitude when the Moon is up.) But another complicating factor for most observers is light pollution. For special consideration of limiting magnitude studies in strongly light-polluted skies, see Activity 59 and Activities 61 and 62.

Let us here assume you have an observing site at which at least the zenith and the lower sky in one direction are not drastically affected by light pollution. When skies are very clear, the limiting magnitudes of stars at different altitudes should conform with the table of values for atmospheric extinction (see Activity 32)—the loss of brightness attributable to air alone. But what about on nights when haze is present? The amount of haze affects how rapidly the brightness falls off with decreasing altitude. Study this!

Different nights will offer drastically different limiting magnitude due to different sky transparency. If you are only seeking the limits of your vision, try only on the obviously clearest, most star-spangled nights. If you are interested also in how transparency varies in different weather situations, try on many nights. If so, you will want to get figures on the temperature and humidity for the time of your observation, along with any other relevant weather information (wind velocity and direction? smog due to an "inversion"?).

Whatever your purposes, you should learn the best ways to see faint objects. Allow your eyes 15 to 30 minutes for *dark adaptation* (a chemical change in the retina) after being in a bright place. You might, in fact, want to test how your limiting magnitude changes 5, 10, 15, 30, or however many minutes after you leave a well-lit room or car. Another key procedure for seeing faint objects is gazing slightly to the side of the dim star you are looking for. This technique of using *averted vision* lets the star's light fall on the most light-sensitive parts of your retina. (For more details and more pointers on seeing dim objects, refer to pages 168 to 173 of my previous book, *The Starry Room.*)

Naturally, you will need star charts with star magnitudes. Figure 6 for summer observers is a start. Others you can make on your own with star atlas and catalog.

The rest of this activity involves comparisons. By checking limiting magnitudes with observers beside you, you can try to discover how much people differ in their ability to see faint stars—and to what extent this difference is a result of age or experience. You can also compare how the daytime indicators of transparency (see Activities 56 and 57) are correlated with the nighttime one of limiting magnitude. (*Warning:* sky transparency can change remarkably quickly, a subject itself worth study.)

Other comparisons? Find out how the limiting magnitude of a pointlike object

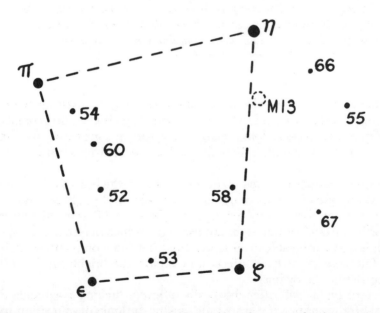

Figure 6 Keystone pattern in constellation Hercules to use for determining limiting magnitude. (Numbers are magnitudes with decimal points omitted— "53" means magnitude 5.3.)

such as a star compares with *extended* objects of various sizes. (For a list of some of these objects, see Activity 30; for discussion of others, Activity 31.) And, finally, how, if at all, are transparency and "seeing" connected? Learn which weather patterns and times of year in your area provide the best of both.

Questions

1. What is your limiting magnitude for stars (and for extended objects) on a moonless night, at a site mostly free of significant light pollution—near the zenith? at lower altitudes? on different nights?

2. To precisely what extent do different weather conditions affect your limiting magnitude? How do your figures for limiting magnitudes correlate with daytime measures of sky transparency?

3. How does your limiting magnitude compare with that of other observers? To what extent are the differences attributable to age, experience, or other causes?

4. Is there any connection between sky transparency and "seeing"? What weather conditions and systems produce the best of both?

28.

Counting Pleiads

Attempt to see as many stars of the Pleiades as possible with the naked eye, and learn how many the average eye usually sees.

The Pleiades is the most famous of star clusters, and the idea of trying to see the greatest number of Pleiads with the naked eye is a very old one. Also ancient is the debate as to how many of these stars can be see by the average naked eye under "average" conditions.

Unfortunately, the attempt to answer these questions has been complicated by considerable confusion.

One confusion involves the visibility of the star Pleione. Figure 7 shows the 9 Pleiad stars with names from Greek mythology, and it also shows that all the stars are magnitude 5.6 or brighter. Seven are named for the Pleiades sisters, the other 2 for the girls' parents, Atlas and Pleione. The latter 2 are separated by only 5 minutes of arc, splittable only with pretty good eyesight and steady atmosphere. Whether an observer could split the pair might determine whether he or she saw 6 or 7 naked-eye Pleiads—we are often told. This might explain the worldwide legend of

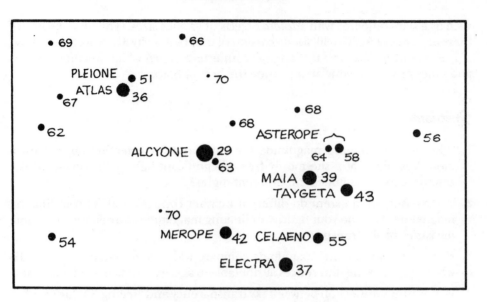

Figure 7 Pleiades star finder chart, with magnitudes (decimal points removed). All stars brighter than 7.0 in this field are shown.

a "lost Pleiad," too, especially along with the fact that Pleione is a decidedly variable star. (In the twentieth century alone, its brightness has varied from magnitude 5.0 to 5.5 and back, apparently due to dimmings by eruptions of gaseous shells.) But any eye capable of seeing Pleione separate would almost surely also notice Celaeno and Asterope. So, unless Pleione was once much brighter, people with rather poor eyes have always been able to see 6 of the main Pleiads and people with slightly better eyes, not 7, but at least 9. The number 7 in this controversy may be due mostly to the fact that there were 7 maidens in the Greek story and also to the special mystical significance of 7 in various influential cultures of ancient times. (By the way, magnitude 5.6 Asterope is actually a double star formed by members of magnitude 5.8 and 6.4, only 2.8 arc-minutes apart. Can anyone without optical aid see these two dim objects as a pair rather than just an elongated form?)

Another confusion, almost never mentioned in discussions of the subject, is the subject of Pleiads too far from the center of the cluster for people to know certainly that they are Pleiads. In Figure 7, the magnitude 5.6 star at upper right and the magnitude 5.4 star at lower left are the outstanding examples that some observers might count and others might not. So far as I know, these two and all others on our chart are indeed Pleiads.

I am not sure if there is any Pleiad conceivably bright enough for the unaided eye that lies beyond the bounds of our chart. But if not—and that is probably true—then this chart presumably does show all the Pleiads that even the best naked eye on the best night could see. The total is 21. But I doubt that the magnitude 6.3 star so near bright Alcyone could ever be glimpsed without optical aid—not even as an elongated form we could count as two, as with Asterope's pair.

Questions

1. How many stars of the Pleiades cluster can you count on a night with average sky conditions? On the best night? Is the best night for this one with best transparency, or does "seeing" also play a role?

2. How many more or less Pleiads can you see than the other people observing with you? Can you split Atlas-Pleione or Asterope?

29.

Observational Tests with M44

Study the naked-eye visibility of M44, the Beehive star cluster, under various sky conditions. With the naked eye, attempt to see a few of its individual stars on excellent nights.

M44, often nicknamed the *Beehive*, is a star cluster in Cancer so prominent that it was well known even in ancient times (when one of its names was Praesepe—"Manger"). The ancients saw only the blended light of its stars and were not aware it was a cluster, calling it the Little Mist or Little Cloud. They—or at least Aratos and Pliny—also wrote of this object's visibility as a weather indicator or predictor.

Today, the cluster's visibility under different sky conditions remains worthy of study; and modern observers can try to make the rare naked-eye observation of individual stars in M44.

M44 seems to be a special favorite of *Sky & Telescope* columnist Walter Scott Houston, and his statements about studying its naked-eye visibility under different conditions can hardly be bettered. On page 188 of the February 1983 *Sky & Telescope,* he writes, "In ancient times M44 was used to forecast the weather. Even the thinnest cirrus clouds, which often signal an approaching front and its attendant storm, render the cluster invisible. It would be a worthwhile project for someone to record the times when M44 is and is not visible to the naked eye, and at the same time the faintest star that is seen nearby. A series of such observations would allow a threshold magnitude to be determined for the cluster's visibility."

With today's improved TV weather coverage, an observer may be able to keep detailed records of factors—amount and kind of cloud, humidity, and so on—that might affect M44's naked-eye visibility. How do different amounts of light pollution affect our seeing M44? If you take such things as light pollution and altitude of the cluster into account, the visibility of M44 becomes (as Houston says in a later

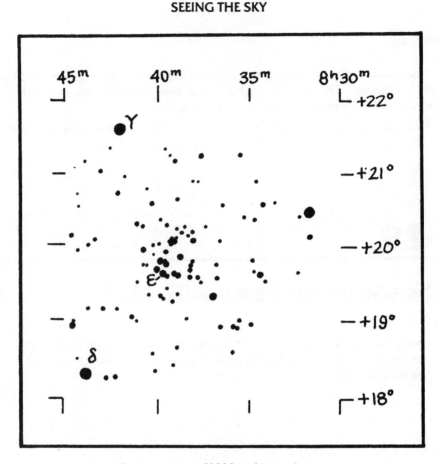

Brightest stars of M44 and its environs.

column) itself a useful observer's guide to the transparency of the sky when planning your night's telescopic observations.

Part 2 of this activity is to achieve a feat that seems at the very limit of unaided vision, perhaps beyond the abilities of many of us: seeing individual stars of the Beehive cluster. In recent years Houston has reported that there are a few records of this observation being made—but the only really modern and well-documented ones he mentions were achieved from a high-flying airplane by a Swedish amateur astronomer and from 9,000 feet up Mauna Kea by eagle-eyed Steve O'Meara.

The problem is not primarily the faintness of the Beehive stars, but their numerousness and crowding. Three Beehive stars are brighter than magnitude 6.5, 11 are brighter than magnitude 6.9, and fully 15 shine between the magnitudes of 6.3 (the brightest member, Epsilon Cancri) and 7.5. Unfortunately, these stars all lie within little more than a degree of each other and have as background scores of fainter cluster members.

The next stage to try for beyond seeing the cluster as merely a fuzzy patch of light is to see it as a patch in which the light is unevenly distributed. It is a beautiful, unique naked-eye sight.

Test your ability to detect this uneven light distribution on various good observing nights. Note in particular how important good seeing is in your attempts to first glimpse this unevenness, and then resolve in it the individual stars.

Questions

1. How does the naked-eye visibility of M44 vary with different sky conditions—including light clouds, humidity, and light pollution? How faint a star, in the sky near the cluster, can be seen when the cluster is invisible? What other large (spread-out) "deep-sky objects" are there whose visibility you can rate in similar fashion?

2. In order to see that light is unevenly spread over the naked-eye fuzzy patch of M44, what must be the limiting magnitude of stars near the cluster? How good is the "seeing"? Can you, on the very best nights, glimpse any of the individual stars of M44 with your naked eye?

30.

Naked-Eye Star Clusters

Observe as many star clusters as possible with the naked eye. Study how sky conditions affect the visibility of clusters that appear as fuzzy patches differently than the way they affect the visibility of points of light.

The Pleiades and the Hyades, the Beehive and Coma Berenices star clusters—most experienced amateur astronomers know that these are naked-eye objects in reasonably good sky conditions. To these clusters might be added a few more, such as the Double Cluster of Perseus, M7 in Scorpius, and M13 in Hercules. But that would exhaust the list of star clusters that most amateur astronomers even realize (let alone have seen for themselves) are visible to the unaided eye.

The amazing truth is that, even in these days of light pollution, many more star clusters can be glimpsed as fuzzy patches of light with the naked eye. In dark country skies, the number could be dozens!

Table 2 is for starters. It does not include a few groupings that have evaded getting an *NGC* (New General Catalog) number or mention in many compilations because of uncertainties as to whether they are true clusters. (The best example is

Table 2
Naked-eye star clusters

Object	Diameter†	Magnitude	Constellation
OPEN CLUSTERS*			
M34	18	5.5	Perseus
NGC 1502	17	5.3	Camelopardalis
M35	40	5.3	Gemini
NGC 2244	40	5.0	Monoceros
NGC 2264	30	4.7	Monoceros
M41	30	5.0	Canis Major
NGC 2353	20	5.3	Monoceros
M47	25	4.5	Puppis
NGC 2451	45	3.6	Puppis
M48	30	5.3	Hydra
NGC 6383	6	5.5	Scorpius
M6	25	5.3	Scorpius
M7	60	3.2	Scorpius
NGC 6633	20	4.9	Ophiuchus
IC 4756	70	5.1	Serpens
M39	30	5.2	Cygnus
IC 1396	50	5.1	Cepheus
GLOBULAR CLUSTERS**			
M3	19	6.4	Canes Venatici
M5	20	6.2	Serpens
M4	23	6.4	Scorpius
M13	23	5.7	Hercules
M92	12	6.1	Hercules
M22	17	5.9	Sagittarius
M55	15	6.0	Sagittarius
M15	12	6.0	Pegasus
M2	12	6.3	Aquarius

* North of −40 degrees and brighter than magnitude 5.5, excluding the Hyades, Pleiades, Beehive, Coma, and Double Clusters.

† Based on photographs; visual size may be considerably smaller.

** North of −40 degrees and brighter than magnitude 6.5.

the very large and bright grouping of stars surrounding Alpha Persei—observe it!) Many clusters dimmer than those on the list are nevertheless perceivable with the naked eye in clear, dark skies.

On the list, start off with the thrill of discovering that the famous M35 in the feet of Gemini is really quite prominent to the naked eye; that more than just one or two globular clusters can be seen (sometimes even several within the same constellation) without optical aid; that the naked eye is one of the best ways to view spread-out M34 in Perseus; that there is a naked-eye star cluster even in dim constellation Camelopardalis!

The naked-eye visibility of star clusters will depend not only on their total brightness but also on how large an area that brightness is spread over. The maximum altitude of the cluster from your latitude, and the distracting stars near it in the sky also have their effect. (Splendid sixth-magnitude M11 would be easier to see with the naked eye if the bright Scutum Star Cloud were not behind it.)

In short, each cluster is a case unto itself, waiting for you to study. If you take note of these different factors, you may be able to determine what the limiting magnitude is for extended objects of various sizes. You can also try to learn at what size you can begin distinguishing a star cluster from a star of similar brightness— on nights of different "seeing." But the greatest satisfaction in this activity should be in observing some of these objects in an interesting way that few other people in the world have done.

Questions

1. How many star clusters in Table 2 can you see with the naked eye in dark skies? In light-polluted skies? Can you see, with the naked eye, other clusters given in my August 1978 article in *Astronomy* magazine or in Phil Harrington's new book *Touring the Universe with Binoculars* (New York: John Wiley & Sons, Inc.)? Can you see clusters not listed in either of these sources?

2. What is the limiting magnitude for clusters of various sizes? Under different seeing conditions, what is the smallest cluster that you can still distinguish as being larger than individual stars?

31.

Other Naked-Eye Deep-Sky Objects

Attempt to see as many deep-sky objects, other than star clusters, as you can with the naked eye. Determine how their combination of brightness and size affects their visibility.

While there are dozens of star clusters that can be detected with the unaided eye, there are far fewer *deep-sky objects* (astronomical objects beyond our solar system) of other kinds that can be. Fortunately, each of the naked-eye *nebulas* and galaxies is extremely distinctive, even more of an individual than most of the clusters.

Nebulas (vast clouds of dust and gas in space) come in several varieties, but the few brightest are *diffuse nebulas* like M42 (the Great Nebula in Orion) and M8 (the Lagoon Nebula). The former presents the naked-eye viewer with the problem of being almost overwhelmed by its proximity to its multiple star Theta Orionis. A very interesting project would be to determine how many people can detect any hint of it around the star with the naked eye under various sky conditions. The Lagoon Nebula in Sagittarius is more impressive with the naked eye than in a very small narrow-field telescope. Tougher possible naked-eye targets in or near Sagittarius include M16 (Eagle or Star-Queen Nebula); M17 (Omega, Checkmark, or Swan Nebula); M20 (Trifid Nebula). Actually these and some other famous nebulas' naked-eye brightness is in part—sometimes in large part—due to star clusters associated with the nebulosity. (The cluster NGC 2237 in Monoceros is easily seen with the naked eye, but its surrounding Rosette Nebula requires potent optical aid.)

Two of the traditionally most difficult nebulas are the California Nebula in Perseus and Barnard's Loop in Orion. But observers using "nebula filters" with naked eye have now succeeded in glimpsing both with this aid—and then the California Nebula without the filter!

Besides the diffuse nebulas (the "swaddling clothes" of stars being born), most amateur astronomers are also familiar with the *planetary nebulas* (the "shrouds" of stars dying). Unfortunately, the brightest planetary nebulas are near the magnitude limit for faint stars, but they are more spread out than stars and hence possess lower surface brightness. Whether anyone can succeed with the naked eye in seeing the magnitude 6.5 but vastly distended Helix Nebula or the much higher surface brightness but only magnitude 7.6 Dumbbell Nebula is an unanswered question.

A final major class of nebulas, the *dark nebulas,* are discussed in Activity 39 in connection with the Milky Way.

And that brings us in our present activity to galaxies other than our own Milky

Way. Observers in the southern hemisphere can, of course, get splendid naked-eye views of the Milky Way's satellite galaxies, the Magellanic Clouds. But at midnorthern latitudes, there are probably just two other galaxies, one easy and one difficult, for naked-eye observation. M31, the very famous Great Andromeda Galaxy, shines at about fourth magnitude. Although this brightness is spread over a several-degree-long area (over 5 degrees long in best naked-eye sightings!), M31 is certainly an easy naked-eye sight in reasonably clear, dark skies. At 2.2 million light-years distant, it is often called the farthest of all naked-eye objects. That title may actually belong, however, to a very slightly farther galaxy, not far from it in the sky—M33. Experienced observers know that M33, at about magnitude 6.5, is indeed visible to the naked eye in very good conditions—despite being spread over more than a degree. Finding how often you can see M33 at all is interesting. For M31, you can determine how much of its length can be detected on various nights. Compare your results with limiting magnitude in this part of the sky.

Questions

1. How many diffuse nebulas (brightness-aided by their clusters) can you detect with the naked eye? Under various sky conditions, how many people can see the Great Nebula in Orion, with the naked eye, despite the light of Theta Orionis?

2. Can any planetary nebula—even the Helix Nebula (NGC 7293) or Dumbbell Nebula (M27)—be glimpsed with the naked eye?

3. How faint must nearby limiting magnitudes of stars be for you to see M33 with the naked eye? How great a length of M31 is visible to the unaided eye under various sky conditions?

32.

Star-Rise, Star-Set, and Atmospheric Extinction

Attempt to see stars (and other celestial objects) of various magnitudes as low in the sky as possible. After making many of these observations, try to correlate your results with meteorological and other sky-affecting conditions.

Is it possible to see a star rise or set right on the distant horizon? Our table of atmospheric extinction (see Table 3) states that even when a star is only 1 degree

Table 3
Atmospheric extinction at various altitudes

Altitude (Degrees)	Dimming (in Magnitudes)
1	3.0
2	2.5
4	2.0
6	1.5
10	1.0
11	0.9
13	0.8
15	0.7
17	0.6
19	0.5
21	0.4
26	0.3
32	0.2
43	0.1

above the horizon, the greater amount of atmosphere it traverses will dim it by just 3 magnitudes. I say "just" because, even though 3 magnitudes is a lot, the figure suggests that any star brighter than about 3rd magnitude (that is, 3 magnitudes above the commonly accepted 6th-magnitude naked-eye limit for faint stars) should be visible to the naked eye 1 degree above the horizon under ideal conditions.

Of course, the catch here is in the word *ideal.* Add dust or moisture—let alone the thinnest of distant clouds—anywhere along that long, earth-grazing line of sight, and the dimming will be greater. I am tempted to claim that it is, in fact, extremely rare for any star—even Sirius, the brightest—to be visible right down to the horizon. But only through attempting this activity can we be sure.

Undoubtedly optical aid could assist in locating a dimmed star precisely for the naked eye. But an attentive naked-eye observer of a sinking star should be able to keep track of its position by using landmarks or higher sky objects as guides.

One experienced observer I know, Steve Albers, feels that in ordinary clear skies the critical altitude below which celestial objects begin to suffer truly severe dimming is 3 degrees. In unusually clear air, the critical altitude would be less. How low would an object have to be for seeing to play a critical role in its visibility?

Here is a final important note: The effects of light pollution at low altitudes is relatively much greater. This current activity can be carried out in a light-polluted sky. The problem is that you will get impressive results—impressively bad.

Questions

1. What is the lowest altitude in the sky at which you can see stars of different magnitudes under various conditions? How do measures of those conditions correlate with your results? What is the lowest altitude at which you can see extended objects of various kinds (bright comets, deep-sky objects, and so on)?

2. At what altitude does dimming of a setting object drastically increase even in a clear sky? Is it similar for different kinds of celestial objects? How much lower is it in an unusually clear sky?

3. At what altitude does "seeing" begin to play an important role in an object's visibility?

33.

Splitting Mizar-Alcor

Find out how good sky transparency and seeing must be before you can discern the star Alcor distinctly beside Mizar. Gather a number of observers together on several occasions, and learn how many of the people are able to split this double star under different sky conditions.

How easy is it for the naked eye to split Mizar and Alcor, the famous close-together pair of stars at the bend of the handle in the Big Dipper? You will read a lot of vague (or sometimes undeservedly precise!) statements on this matter in astronomy books. But you will not read of anyone having actually put this question to a proper test.

Mizar and Alcor are separated by 11.8 arc-minutes. Since this is more than one-third the apparent diameter of the Moon, you would think that no one with normal eyesight could fail to split the pair. But the problem is not splitting per se. As in so many other such observations, the difficulty comes from a much brighter object distracting the eye from the fainter. The magnitudes of Mizar and Alcor are 2.4 and 4.0, respectively—not a huge difference, but still substantial.

One of the medieval Arabic names for Alcor means "The Test," but the question is whether seeing Alcor was considered a test of a person's having superb eyesight or simply normal vision. Presumably the latter is true (though in those days before eyeglasses, just to have 20/20 vision must have been much esteemed). But only by experiment can we be more sure.

After you have tried spotting Alcor yourself on various occasions, gather a group of observers together for the attempt several times under different sky conditions. You may wish to learn from each individual whether he or she has previous background in trying this observation or even in trying astronomy in general. A person who knows where Alcor lies with respect to Mizar may find it hard to keep from being biased (not to mention aided) by this knowledge.

Questions

1. How easily can you spot Alcor with the naked eye under different sky conditions?

2. What percentage of people that you test together are able to see Alcor with the naked eye under different sky conditions? Does bias from previous experience or knowledge make a difference?

34.

Splitting Other Double Stars

Try splitting as many double stars as you can with the naked eye. Determine how much various magnitudes and magnitude differences between members of a pair affect your ability to split them. Test how seeing and transparency affect your ability to split them. Find what double star is the closest pairing your naked eye can split under excellent conditions and what double star is the closest pairing splittable by other people.

A *double star* is any star that, upon (further) examination, is found to consist of two or more stars. A double star may be an *optical double*—a pair in which one star is much farther and merely lying on the same line of sight as the other member. Or, more commonly, a double star may be a true *binary*, in which the two suns move through space together about a common center of gravity.

The distance between components of a double star is small compared with their distance from us. Consequently, most double stars require the magnification of a telescope before they are "split"—that is to say, before the apparent gap between the two component stars is great enough for us to see them as separate points of light.

There are, however, a small number of double stars that can be or might be split with the naked eye. (See Table 4.) It is not a very large sampling upon which to base universal conclusions about the limits of human visual acuity, especially

Table 4
Naked-eye double stars

	Magnitudes	Separation*
Mizar-Alcor	2.4, 4.0	11'48"
Alpha Capricorni	3.6, 4.2	6'16"
Mu Scorpii	3.1, 3.6	5'46"
Alpha Librae	2.7, 5.2	3'51"
Epsilon Lyrae	5.0, 5.1	3'30"
16, 17 Draconis**	5.2, 5.6	1'30"
Nu Draconis**	5.0, 5.0	1'02"

* In minutes and seconds of arc
** May be too difficult for even the sharpest naked eyes

considering how many variables can affect one's results. But the object of this activity is to try to isolate those variables and draw at least some conclusions, while also enjoying the experience of observing each double star and dealing with it as a case unto itself.

Variables include different sky conditions of darkness, transparency, and seeing, and different levels of visual acuity in various people. The brightnesses of the component stars and the amount of *difference* between their brightnesses are other factors; the brighter a star, the easier it is to see; the less difference in brightness between the two, the easier the fainter star is to see.

The attempter of this activity should therefore (1) rate "seeing" and limiting magnitude in the part of the sky around the double star (see Activities 26 and 27) and (2) bring together a number of people to attempt the splits so that the role of individual visual acuity can be assessed.

Questions

1. How many double stars can you split with the naked eye? How good does "seeing" and limiting magnitude have to be for a pair of given separation to be split?

2. How much closer together can a pair of equally bright stars be and still be as splittable as a farther-apart double star in which the components are two (or three) magnitudes different?

3. Under excellent conditions, what is the closest double star you can split with your naked eye? What is the closest double star other people can split under the same observing conditions?

35.

Betelgeuse and Similar Variable Stars

*Estimate as often as possible the brightness of Betelgeuse and the other
semiregular or irregular red giant variable stars easily visible to the naked eye.*

Betelgeuse is the brightest "red" (really more like golden orange) star and reddest bright star in the heavens. It may also be the largest star visible to the naked eye. With these and other remarkable distinctions and its prominent place in the brilliant constellation Orion, you would think that Betelgeuse's sometimes large variations in brightness would be monitored by many people. Not so!

The only popular article I know of that has encouraged watching Betelgeuse's variations is one in the February 1983 issue of *Sky & Telescope*. In that article, Joseph Ashbrook's observations show mostly slight, gradual variations of Betelgeuse, but also some sizable changes occurring rapidly. (For instance, a remarkable rise, then fall, of 0.4 magnitude in about two weeks occurred in February 1957.) Ashbrook's extreme values for the star between 1937 and 1975 were magnitudes −0.1 and +1.1.

Of course, obtaining accurate estimates of this star requires some special effort. Betelgeuse is so bright that suitable comparison stars must be sought quite a distance away in the sky. Consequently, you must record the exact time of observation (or altitude of the stars used) so that you can figure the amounts the different stars were dimmed by atmospheric extinction at their various altitudes. (See Table 3.) You must also look out for both Moon and city sky glow reducing the stars' observed brightness more in one part of the sky than in another. This is especially tricky when light pollution is involved. Activities 8 and 59 can help you determine the dimming effects of both Moon and light pollution for various times and locations, but observing the stars in question at several different times of night may offer a quick solution that suffices. (How dimmed is Betelgeuse when it gets to about where its comparison star, Aldebaran, was in city sky glow?) Making brightness estimates several times a night is a good check on yourself regardless.

The problems with getting suitable comparison stars are even greater for Antares, but far less for the dimmer stars in our activity. All these red giants in this activity are *semiregular* or *irregular* variable stars. That means they offer surprises galore but also hope of establishing certain patterns in their variations.

Here are notes on ranges and periods (of time from one maximum to the next). For Betelgeuse and Antares, no finder charts are needed. (Any basic star map shows them and their comparison stars.)

Betelgeuse (Alpha Orionis). Extreme range about −0.1 to about +1.5. Periods: main period about 5.7 years, superimposed secondary period of roughly

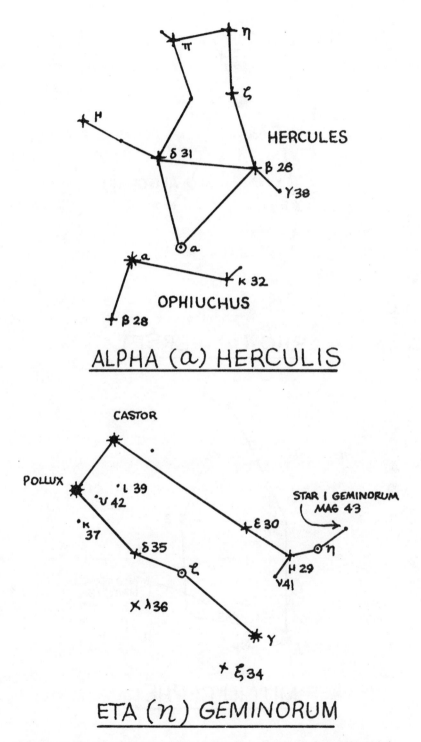

ALPHA (α) HERCULIS

ETA (η) GEMINORUM

Some variable stars (decimal point omitted in magnitude figures by stars).

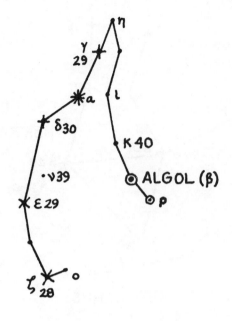

RHO (ρ) PERSEI

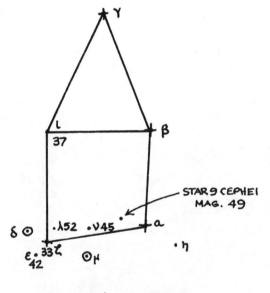

MU (μ) CEPHEI

150 to 300 days. Comparison stars: Capella (0.08); Rigel (0.12, though slightly variable itself); Procyon (0.38); Aldebaran (0.85); Pollux (1.14); Castor (1.59); Bellatrix (Gamma Orionis) (1.64).

Antares (Alpha Scorpii). Variations very seldom studied. Typical range is often given as barely perceptible, from about 0.86 to 1.06; but extreme dimness recorded is 1.8. Period: about 4.75 years. Comparison stars: Altair (0.77); Spica (1.00, very slightly variable); Deneb (1.26); Lambda Scorpii (1.62); Epsilon Sagittarii (1.81). Note that the first three, the ones most used, are very far from Antares.

Rasalgethi (Alpha Herculis). Extreme range about 3.0 to 3.9. Periods: very, very roughly, 90 days; possibly about 6 years.

Propus (Eta Geminorum). Range about 3.3 to 3.9 (and slightly fainter). Period: about 233 days.

Rho Persei. Range about 3.3 to 4.0. Periods: roughly 33 to 40 days; 3.5 years. Neighbor in sky of most famous variable star, Algol.

Mu Cephei. Range about 3.7 to 5.0. Periods: about 100 days; very roughly 755 days. (A longest period of about 12.8 years also suspected!)

Questions

1. What is the current brightness of all the variable stars in this activity? How much are they changing this week and this month?
2. How long are the periods you find for these stars, and how do these figures compare with the statistics for them given above?
3. By comparing your brightness estimates of a reddish star like Betelgeuse and a white or blue star with those of another observer, can you determine a greater red-light sensitivity for one of you?

36.

Identifying Constellations

Identify as many constellations as possible with the naked eye by locating all their stars brighter than at least magnitude 5.0 (5.5 in the case of a few very faint constellations).

Some astronomy books still mention the constellations as things of interest in their own rights. But do any champion the goal of identifying as many constellations and their patterns as possible?

Lots of amateur astronomers with telescopes today try to locate and observe all of the 110 *deep-sky objects* on Charles Messier's list. Why shouldn't we also look for the 88 constellations (or as many of them as we can see from our latitude)? Are you any less accomplished an observer for not having seen M76 (the Little Dumbbell Nebula in Perseus) than for not having seen Crater (the Cup) or for not knowing exactly where to find M104 (the Sombrero Galaxy) than for not knowing exactly where to find Camelopardalis (the Giraffe)?

The constellations should be territories of the heavens that come alive for the observer, each with its individual character (and its own lode of myth and lore, too). And it is of practical benefit to know your way around the heavens without having to refer every minute to your star charts.

Of course, to take on this activity of seeing as many constellations as possible, you will need a star atlas or some kind of star maps to begin with. If you do not have one and do not wish to buy one, there is always the library. When is the last time you knowingly looked at some of the less famous constellations—or have you ever? Have you ever traced the patterns of their main stars? If you observe from a site where light pollution is even slightly bad, you will have a tough time with the dimmest of these constellations. But to truly say you have seen each in detail, you really should identify all their stars brighter than magnitude 5.0, or, in the case of the faintest constellations, magnitude 5.5!

Questions

1. In how many constellations can you observe all stars brighter than magnitude 5.0? What is the most difficult constellation, wholly above −35 degrees declination, to identify in this way from your (midnorthern latitude) observing location?

2. By checking out the depictions of the figures (twins, ram, hunter, winged horse, and so on) in old star atlases (or in recent reproductions of them) or by referring to a book like R. H. Allen's *Star Names: Their Lore and Meaning* (New York: Dover Publications, Inc.), can you learn what each part of a star pattern you observe is traditionally supposed to represent?

37.

Identifying and Discovering Asterisms

Identify all the traditional asterisms you can. Then find (and, if you wish, name) asterisms of your own.

An *asterism* is a pattern of stars that does not form the main or full pattern of any constellation now officially recognized. That does not mean that all asterisms are little known. The Big Dipper is perhaps the most famous of all star patterns (in the United States at least), yet it is an asterism, just a part of the larger pattern of the official constellation Ursa Major, the Great Bear.

On the other hand, few people today know of the asterism called the Diamond of Venus or know that Orion the Hunter has not only Belt, Sword, Club, and Shield but also Bow (in one medieval Arabic imagining). The search for these asterisms increases one's familiarity with the starry heavens. And what do you do after you have found some of the traditional asterisms? Then the search for ones of your own even more greatly enhances your knowledge of the starry sky and provides some interesting new sights.

Table 5 lists some of the more notable traditional asterisms. Some are very famous; others are now observed by (or even known to) exceedingly few people. Locate the component stars mentioned first on a star chart, then in the heavens themselves.

You will find that some of these asterisms—like the Summer Triangle—are quite large and extend across the boundaries of several official constellations. On the other hand, others—like the Water Jar, or Urn—are quite compact, obviously having drawn attention by their seeming to be curious little *gatherings* of stars.

Your search for "new" asterisms of your own will tend to find large, inter-constellational ones, on moonlit or partly cloudy nights when certain bright stars stand out, and small intra-constellational ones, on clear nights.

Why is it not necessarily the clearest nights when certain small asterisms of faint stars are seen? Because asterisms of 4th- and 5th-magnitude stars may actually be less prominent when their background is crowded with 5th- and 6th-magnitude stars! The wonderful fact is that every level of sky darkness and transparency presents most prominently a whole different set of asterisms. And by the way, "seeing" also plays a role. An extremely compact asterism of a few faint stars (for instance, the one on the line between Epsilon and Iota Cassiopeiae) will, on a night of poor seeing, look more like a fuzzy patch to the naked eye—initially fooling you into thinking this could be a true, even a rich, cluster.

Table 5
Some interesting asterisms

The Big Dipper	In Ursa Major
The Little Dipper	Main pattern of Ursa Minor
The Lozenge	The head of Draco
The Kids	In Auriga
The Winter Hexagon*	Aldebaran, Capella, Castor and Pollux, Procyon, Sirius, Rigel
The False Cross	Epsilon and Iota Carinae, Kappa and Delta Velorum
The Sickle	In Leo
The Three Leaps of the Gazelle	Iota and Kappa, Lambda and Mu, Nu and Xi Ursae Majoris
The Diamond of Venus	Beta Leonis, Alpha Canes Venatici, Arcturus, Spica
The Keystone	In Hercules (see figure on page 54)
The Fish-hook	Sting of Scorpius
The Summer Triangle	Vega, Deneb, Altair
The Northern Cross	Main pattern of Cygnus the Swan
The Teapot	Of Sagittarius
The Milk Dipper	Some of the Teapot's stars: Lambda (handle-end) and Sigma, Tau, Zeta, Phi (bowl) in Sagittarius
Urn or Water Jar	Of Aquarius
Great Square of Pegasus	Also a baseball diamond
The Circlet	Western head of Pisces
The Southern Cross	Main pattern of Crux the Cross

* Instead of drawing the final line from Rigel to Aldebaran, draw it from Rigel to Betelgeuse and you have "the Heavenly G."

Questions

1. How many of the traditional asterisms can you observe? Can you invent any large asterisms that are really striking or in some way stand in helpful or beautiful relation to other parts of the heavens?

2. How many compact asterisms of faint stars can you find the next time you observe in a quite dark, clear sky? How do different seeing conditions affect what your compact asterism looks like? At what level of sky transparency and darkness—and with what limiting magnitude in its area—does your asterism stand out most prominently?

38.

Visibility of the Milky Way

Rate the visibility or prominence of different parts of the Milky Way on various nights. Compare your rating to limiting magnitude figures and meteorological statistics to see what correlations exist.

We live in a vast galaxy of roughly several hundred billion stars called the Milky Way. But the "the Milky Way" is also a band of soft light that runs around the heavens, appearing most prominent in certain stretches of constellations. The latter Milky Way is the combined glow of millions of stars that appear as a band in our sky because we are located in the same plane as they are—the star-crowded central or equatorial plane of our Milky Way Galaxy. (See Figure 8.)

Interestingly, the visibility of the Milky Way band seems to vary somewhat differently under different sky conditions than individual faint stars do. What is surprising is that individual faint stars seem to suffer from a slight haze more than the extended glow of the Milky Way does. If I am right, however, how much haze is the right amount to produce this effect? The full description of the matter is more complex than the statement I have made. And the only way to get the full answers is by a series of careful observations.

What kinds of observations are needed? As with most celestial objects, the visibility of the Milky Way is significantly reduced by light pollution and haze—both of which can make the normal dimming that occurs low in the sky far more severe. To gauge these, the observer should make limiting magnitude estimates and write down statistics on relevant weather conditions, just as in a number of our earlier activities. But here there are a few more complications. Parts of the Milky Way band are far brighter than others. Furthermore, you should do limiting magnitude estimates at the same altitude as, but not right in the midst of, a bright section of the Milky Way band. (Its glow generally makes it more difficult to see the faintest individual stars.)

The final factor that complicates this activity is the fact that the Milky Way glow ultimately is granular, with some of the "grains"—that is, individual stars—being bright enough to glimmer on the limits of individual naked-eye vision. What this means for the visibility of the Milky Way forces us to define the term *visibility* more carefully. We can speak of three separate aspects of visibility that can easily be confused together, but that should be kept separate: (1) how bright the brighter portions of the Milky Way seem; (2) how much detail (in the different gradations of brightness) is discernible; and (3) how extensive are the areas of sky across which the width of the Milky Way band is able to be seen. I think we will find that these three aspects are not necessarily going to vary exactly the same as one another.

Make aspect 1 of the Milky Way's visibility the goal of this activity—how bright the brighter portions of the Milky Way seem. I say "seem" because the only way the

Figure 8 Overhead and side view of Milky Way, showing approximate position of our solar system.

eye itself can gauge the brightness of such vastly extended areas is by estimating the prominence with which the glows stand out against a dark sky. Our old 0 to 10 scale can be your starting point. And as for Milky Way visibility aspects 2 and 3—they are the subjects of our next two activities, which you should try in connection with the present activity.

Questions

1. On a 0 to 10 scale, how prominently bright against the night sky are the brighter sections of the Milky Way tonight? (Each bright section may deserve its own rating.)

2. What are the effects of factors—like low altitude in the sky, haze, and light pollution—on the Milky Way brightness, in terms of your scale correlated with measures of these factors (like weather statistics and limiting magnitude)? On the basis of limiting magnitude estimates and your Milky Way scale, do you find that the Milky Way's prominence seems less decreased by a little haze than by that of individual stars?

39.

Levels of Brightness in the Milky Way

Note the amount of structure—that is, structure in the gradations of brightness—visible in the Milky Way on different nights. Relate it to sky conditions and weather conditions, but also to your ratings of Milky Way brightness (see the previous activity) and extent (see the next activity). Make maps of the structure that, including dark areas, your naked eye perceives along the Milky Way.

What a marvelously intricate river of light the Milky Way is on some nights! But the portrayal of it in star atlases is usually only one- or two-toned and sometimes not even based on visual studies. There have been few illustrations that come close to matching what the careful eye sees of the Milky Way on excellent nights.

That is the object of this activity, pure and simple: to make such sketches. But once again, it is important to note light pollution, haze, weather information, limiting magnitude figures, and the like for the time of your drawing. You should also mark down your rating of the bright Milky Way sections' prominence from our previous activity. And our next activity pays special attention to what would be the very lightest pencil-brushed areas in your sketches—the most peripheral reaches of the visible band. What conclusions can you form from relating your drawings and prominence ratings to various conditions? Perhaps you can find whether (as I suspect) very good nights for Milky Way structure or extent are not always the best for bright Milky Way prominence, and why this is so.

I would argue that the granular nature of the Milky Way glow that I alluded to in the previous activity is partly responsible. That keen and knowing observer Walter Scott Houston has noted that, on the very best of nights in darkest skies, the Milky Way clouds begin to break up into the individual glitters of their sixth- and seventh-magnitude stars. Of course, these are only the brightest of the stars that make up the glow, so presumably the process is never complete. But the varying extent to which it occurs—not just varying on different nights but in different parts of the Milky Way band—must play a role in the visibility of structure as well as in the other aspects of Milky Way visibility.

As examples of the wonders you will see, let us consider just a few of the largest or most striking features of the Milky Way band in the glorious stretch from Cygnus to Sagittarius. The major star clouds of Cygnus, Scutum, and Sagittarius dominate the view, along with the striking Rift—a split in the Milky Way along this entire section which leaves one branch of the Milky Way to trickle to its end in northern Ophiuchus. But other dark bays exist—for instance, the prominent but seldom-mentioned one that cuts deep into the Milky Way band north of Deneb—and there are a few naked-eye dark nebulas that are not too difficult to identify. Of these latter objects, the most famous is the Coalsack of the Southern Cross, properly visible only in the tropics and southern hemisphere. But naked-eye viewers all over the world can see the Pipe Nebula of Barnard, whose stem and bowl extends for about 7 degrees near Theta Ophiuchi. Patches of especially bright star cloud will draw your attention far more readily than any dark areas, though. The most intense knot of light is M24, sometimes called the Small Sagittarius Star Cloud. It measures only about 2 degrees by 1 degree.

Questions

1. How much structure in the Milky Way can you see and sketch on various nights? Precisely how is the amount of detectable structure related to various sky and weather conditions? (Will a certain structure be invisible if the limiting magnitude in its area is not better than, say, magnitude 5.5, or if the humidity at the time is not less than 60 percent?)

2. On a given night, what is the relation between your prominence ratings from Activity 38 and the amount of structure you see? How many individual features and how many different gradations of brightness can you distinguish at one session?

40.

Greatest Extent of the Milky Way

In dark, clear skies, attempt to see as great an extent of the Milky Way as possible.

The prime goal of this activity is not to see the Milky Way band extending as near to the horizon as possible, although that is a fine additional goal to seek. Here we are primarily concerned with seeing as much width as possible to parts of the band—beholding Milky Way glow out to its very faintest peripheral extensions.

There is probably no simple criterion we could use to judge exactly at what distance from the equatorial plane of the Milky Way that stars distant from Earth are too few to combine and create a glow. Parts of the Milky Way band differ (in their distance from us and in their richness of stars), eyes and observing ability differ, observing conditions differ. The only way to learn how extensive an area over which the human eye can detect Milky Way glow is to have a lot of people look and find out.

You will need very clear, dark skies. You will need to use "averted vision" to see the faintest radiance possible. You will need to check yourself to be sure you really are seeing glow where you think you are.

What are areas you should especially examine? The northern Ophiuchus tongue of the Milky Way. The constellation Lyra. (Do you see the faintest peripheral Milky Way reaching it? how far into it?) Almost anywhere along the band may hold treasure of subtlest Milky Way extensions previously unrealized. Walter Scott Houston has spoken of a superb night on which he could see Milky Way extend as far in the sky as to reach near M31, the Great Galaxy in Andromeda.

Questions

1. To how great a distance from the central line of the Milky Way band can you see Milky Way glow on excellent nights?

2. Are the nights when the greatest extent of glow is visible the same as those with greatest Milky Way prominence (see Activity 38) or most Milky Way structure (see Activity 39)? What sky and weather conditions exist on the nights of greatest Milky Way extent?

3. How near to the horizon can you see the Milky Way glow on different nights?

41.

Most Southerly Stars and Constellations from Your Latitude

Observe the most southerly (or, if you live in the southern hemisphere, the most northerly) stars and constellations you can from your homesite. Do the same when you travel to other latitudes.

If you want to enjoy and know the starry heavens to the fullest extent possible, you have to look at the whole sky. And that includes the southern limits of it, low in the south sky, where stars peek above the horizon for only a fairly brief time. Even though haze, light pollution, and plain atmospheric extinction decrease the brightness of objects seen so low, some of these celestial sights actually can appear more prominent than most amateur astronomers think. And even to get a mere glimpse is exciting if that object happens to be something like the second brightest star in all the heavens visible from Earth!

The second brightest star is Canopus, and it can be viewed with ease from the southernmost United States. What a sign of 40-degrees-north chauvinism it is that most astronomy books treat this star as if it were a stranger. Many millions of people in the United States can see it plainly! Of course, the catch is that—with Canopus or any very southerly object, you have to know just when to look to get a proper view.

The right time is as near as possible to the time of its *culmination*. A star (or any object) culminates when it reaches the *meridian*—the line that bisects the sky by running from due south through the zenith to due north. When a star culminates, it is at its highest possible point for an observer at that latitude. (The only exception is circumpolar stars at "lower culmination.")

Table 6 gives the dates on which certain interesting southerly stars and other objects culminate at 9:00 P.M. local standard time. You can determine other dates and times for when these culminations occur—and for when other stars and constellations culminate—with a *planisphere* (sometimes called a "star finder") or with charts in various books and astronomy magazines.

Now you might think that observations would not be needed to determine how far north Canopus, or the Southern Cross, or other objects can be glimpsed. Couldn't calculations give us the answers? It is true that you can find the *declination* (equivalent of latitude in the heavens) of any object in a star atlas and figure whether ideally it would be visible from your latitude on Earth: The figure for the declination of your southern horizon is your latitude minus 90 degrees. (Thus at latitude 40 degrees north on Earth, the declination of the southern horizon should be 40 minus 90 equals negative 50—that is, −50 degrees declination.) But this first

Table 6
Culminating dates for some famous southerly objects
(9:00 P.M. standard time)

Canopus	Second brightest star	Feb 11
Eta Carinae	Great nebula, variable star	Apr 17
Southern Cross	Famous asterism, constellation	May 15
Omega Centauri	Brightest globular cluster	Jun 2*
Alpha Centauri	Nearest star, third brightest	Jun 16
Achernar	Ninth brightest star, River's end	Nov 30

* Approximate

calculation gives you only the ideal horizon. Your real horizon may be worse or, if you are observing from a mountain or from a higher elevation of some kind, a little better. More importantly, you would have to figure how low in the sky a given object could be before atmospheric extinction would render it too faint to see. And any light pollution or haze (which varies much from night to night) would alter that figure to extents hard to calculate.

The bottom line is that only you the observer can prove what is the most southerly celestial object you can see from your latitude (or from any other you visit). And it may be you who first proves that the Southern Cross, Alpha Centauri, Omega Centauri, or some other great sky wonder of the southern heavens can be seen, not just in theory, but also in practice from your latitude and location.

Questions

1. What southerly objects (on our list and otherwise) can you observe from your homesite and from other latitudes you visit?
2. What is the most southerly celestial object of all you can glimpse from home and from other latitudes?

42.

Co-Risers, Co-Setters, and Rise-Set Pairs

Identify what stars (and other celestial objects) rise at the same time, set at the same time, or form rise-set pairs (one object rising while the other is setting) as seen from your latitude. Identify what pairs of bright stars or constellations can never be seen above the horizon at the same time from your latitude.

One of the twentieth century's greatest amateur astronomers, Leslie Peltier, noted that the bright stars Capella and Fomalhaut rose around the same time, as seen from his home in Delphos, Ohio. This relationship between the two stars is interesting because Fomalhaut is over 6 hours of right ascension (one-fourth the way west around the heavens) west of Capella. The catch is that this advantage of Fomalhaut's in the contest as to which star rises first is almost exactly offset by Capella's advantage in being so much farther north than Fomalhaut—as seen by an observer around 40 degrees north latitude.

Peltier spent more time and gained more familiarity with the stars than almost anyone ever has. Was his awareness (and obvious delight) in noting co-risers like Capella and Fomalhaut a result of his knowledge of the heavens, or was it a cause of it? Both, you might say. What is clear is that, once again, this activity—to see co-risers, co-setters, and rise-set pairs—is one that anyone who really wants to know and enjoy the heavens should try.

What stars have these relations with each other varies very much from one latitude to another (especially over the narrow range of latitudes when a star goes from being almost circumpolar to circumpolar). Of course, the rise and set times for any celestial objects at any latitude can be calculated, and thus, which relationships exist between which stars can be identified for wherever you live. (Steve Albers and I have, in fact, begun work on producing this data in the most useful form possible for those interested in these questions.) But even if you have the data, you should go out and see the sights for yourself.

It is also true that a rise-set pair in which the riser really comes above the horizon at almost exactly the minute the setter goes below the horizon is going to be next to impossible to see (that is, to see both stars at the same time) because of atmospheric extinction rendering both invisible when they are less than a few degrees above the horizon. There should be at least a few minutes after the time one rises before the other sets. The practical step of observation is necessary to determine whether enough minutes separate the two events—whether the sight actually can be seen.

Perhaps the most interesting of all rise-set pairs is Betelgeuse and Antares. These are the two preeminently visible red giant stars in the heavens, but one reigns in winter and the other in summer. There is even a legend that their two constellations, Orion and Scorpius, are archenemies—the Scorpion having stung and killed the Hunter in their earthly lives—so that now Orion leaves the sky whenever Scorpius is about to appear. But any two stars must be visible above the horizon at the same time from some parts of the world. Check to see if Antares and Betelgeuse can be glimpsed together from your latitude. You will have to have an unobstructed view down to the horizon in the west and the southeast if you want to try this from midnorthern latitudes. There is less distance westward from Antares to Betelgeuse, so the time to look is when the former is rising and the latter, setting—preferably in the midst of a clear country night.

Questions

1. What pairs of stars or other celestial objects rise at the same time, set at the same time, or form a rise-set pair (one rising as the other sets) as seen from your latitude?

2. Can you see Betelgeuse and Antares above the horizon at the same time from your latitude? If not, can you identify other pairs of stars that can never be seen up at the same time from your latitude?

43.

Extreme Width of Celestial Field of View

Determine what are the widest horizontal and the widest vertical separations between bright celestial objects over which your fixed naked eye can still perceive both objects. Then, learn what are the farthest-apart objects of fainter magnitudes that can both be fit within your fixed gaze, horizontally and vertically. Finally, find out the widest fields of view over which you can see celestial objects sharply—with sharply *defined in several different degrees of resolving ability.*

In my earlier book, *The Starry Room,* I discussed the normal and extreme limits to the vertical and horizontal widths of people's naked-eye field of view. One fact mentioned is that there appear to be some individuals with markedly better peripheral vision and wider field of view than other people.

Table 7
Extreme widths of naked-eye fields of view
(in degrees)*

	Theoretical Norm	*Exceptional* **
Horizontal	180	195
Vertical	112	140
Up	47	70
Down	65	70

* With eyes looking directly straight ahead

** Then basketball star, now U.S. Senator, Bill Bradley
(as described in John McPhee's *A Sense of Where You
Are*)

To see where you fall in this range of variation is interesting in itself, for more than just astronomical purposes. But this activity also increases your awareness of your natural optical instruments' powers and brings greater areas of sky than you would normally attend to (in one view) into your consciousness.

Of course, the human eye can scan across most of the starry sky quite quickly, and a few moves of the head or body can permit you to survey all of the heavens in a matter of seconds. But it is interesting to know just how large a group of constellations your vision can hold, and can hold within a field of reasonably sharp vision, in a single view. Can all the bright constellations of the Winter Host (Orion, Taurus, Auriga, Gemini, Canis Minor, and Canis Major) be seen in the same view sharply? (If so, down to what magnitude can they be seen?) Can all three stars of the Summer Triangle (Vega, Deneb, and Altair) be seen sharply together at once? You will need to define *sharply* in terms of being able to distinguish close-together stars separately, and so on. You can have several different degrees of sharpness that you test yourself for.

Table 7 gives the theoretical norms for field of view (in tests in the optometrist's office) plus the far better than normal values of one individual (present U.S. Senator and former college and professional star basketball player, Bill Bradley).

Questions

1. What are the vertical and horizontal limits to the width of your fixed naked-eye field of view, as measured in terms of your ability to detect, both at once, very widely separated celestial objects in the sky? What are the limits on your field of view for fainter celestial objects of various magnitude levels?

2. Which famous groupings of constellations (or, in the case of long Hydra, what constellation!) can you not quite see all of in one fixed gaze? Which can you see with various degrees of sharpness?

44.

Heliacal Risings and Settings of Stars

Observe the earliest (calendar date) heliacal risings and latest (calendar date) heliacal settings of various stars. Note how sky conditions affect the dates at which these sightings can be made.

Helios is Greek for the Sun, so the *heliacal rising* of a star ought to be its rising at exactly the same time as the Sun. In practice, however, heliacal rising has come to mean the first rising of a star long enough before sunrise to be visible.

We say "first" rising because all stars rise about four minutes earlier each day due to the Earth's motion in its orbit around the Sun. (It is our angle of perspective in relation to the stars and Sun that changes.)

Yet another piece of terminology to make clear is the "rising" and "setting": Here we are not attempting to see a star, however bright, right on the horizon. (As we discussed in Activity 32, this is exceedingly difficult even in a fully dark sky.) *Rising* must mean "briefly visible low in the east before dawn gets too bright," and *setting* must mean "briefly visible low in the west after dusk ceases being too bright."

Now for the attraction, even mystique, of this activity.

The watch for the first heliacal rising of certain stellar objects was of crucial importance to some past societies. The most famous case is that of Sirius, whose heliacal rising occurs at the time of the annual life-giving flooding of the Nile—so critical an event that it marked the beginning of the New Year in ancient Egypt. No wonder the Egyptians were moved by the sight of Sirius returning. But even to today's observer, that first glimpse of the brightest star beyond our solar system, glimmering in the dawn light, is inherently inspiring.

As the by far brightest star, Sirius remains a great target of today's watchers of heliacal risings. But the date at which it first becomes visible in bright morning twilight does not just vary according to sky conditions and your observing ability: it also varies according to your latitude. This is a function of how steeply it ascends the sky at that time of year as seen from your latitude. And that steepness will, for most objects seen from middle latitudes on Earth, be different for the heliacal setting than the heliacal rising. Thus, for instance, Sirius lingers longer in invisibility from the time of heliacal setting until it reaches "conjunction" (due south of the Sun) than it does from conjunction until heliacal rising.

Table 8 lists the dates when various bright stars are at conjunction with the Sun each non-leap year. Then it gives—for 40 degrees north latitude—the dates on which they rise at the same time as the Sun and the dates on which they rise 1 hour before the Sun. The date of first dawn visibility—of heliacal rising—should, for all bright stars, fall between these two latter dates. You must find it for yourself by

Heliacal rising of Sirius in ancient Egypt.

Table 8
Information for observing heliacal risings*

Object(s)	Conjunction with Sun	Rises with Sun**	Rises 1 Hour Before Sun**
Alpha, Beta Capricorni	Jan 22	Jan 15	Feb 7
Alpha Andromedae	Mar 23	Feb 1	Mar 1
Pleiades	May 20	May 16	Jun 3
Aldebaran	Jun 1	Jun 7	Jun 22
Betelgeuse	Jun 20	Jul 2	Jul 16
Pollux	Jul 17	Jul 10	Jul 25
Procyon	Jul 16	Jul 27	Aug 9
Sirius	Jul 2	Aug 4	Aug 15
Regulus	Aug 21	Aug 21	Sep 2
Arcturus	Oct 29	Oct 7	Oct 20
Spica	Oct 16	Oct 17	Oct 29
Antares	Dec 1	Dec 7	Dec 18
Altair	Jan 15	Dec 15	Dec 27

* The *heliacal rising*—the first dawn visibility of the object—should occur (weather permitting) sometime between the dates in the last two columns.

** For 40 degrees north latitude.

observation. (Viewers at other latitudes, or of other objects, will have to go it even more on their own.)

Of course, hazy (not to mention cloudy) skies can postpone your first sighting of the heliacal riser or make less late the last sighting of your heliacal setter. Note carefully this factor each year you try the activity on any given star or other celestial object.

Questions

1. What are the heliacal rising and setting dates of the stars you observe?

2. How much can hazy skies alter the dates of heliacal rising and setting for you?

45.

Daytime and Bright Twilight Visibility of Stars

With the naked eye, try to observe the very brightest stars when the Sun is still slightly above the horizon. Try to observe stars of the various less bright magnitudes as early in dusk or as late in dawn as possible. Make special efforts to see selected objects of importance—Polaris, the Pleiades, and so on— as early in dusk or as late in dawn as you can.

I know of several cases, past and present, of naked-eye observers seeing zero-magnitude stars, like Arcturus and Vega, with the Sun still just above the horizon. I suspect that a person may not have to be keen-eyed to achieve this remarkable observation, merely patient and industrious. And the work involved is greatly lessened (as well as your chances improved), if you observe around sunrise and have only to keep the star you are already watching in sight.

Needless to say, the sky should be very clear (a deep blue by day) if you want to achieve the most impressive results possible. Of course, it is also rewarding to see what is typically the point in twilight when a star of a certain brightness becomes visible. Stars of each rank of magnitude will come out at their appointed times in twilight, and you may find it surprising how early you can first glimpse them once you learn exactly where to look. Remember (as when looking for Venus in broad daylight) that you must make sure your eyes are focused far enough away. Note both the time and the date when you glimpse the stars. What really counts is the *solar depression angle* (s.d.a.)—how far the Sun is below the horizon—and this varies with latitude and time of year. But if you have the time of day and the date (plus the latitude of your observing site), the s.d.a. can be calculated later.

Naturally, it is interesting to see how early or late in twilight special celestial objects like the Pleiades star cluster or the Great Galaxy in Andromeda can be spotted with the unaided eye. But there is one star in particular that is not just interesting but is also easier to locate than others—the North Star, Polaris.

Once you have, at night, fixed the position of Polaris above a treetop or a neighbor's antenna (as seen from a certain spot—say, in your front yard), you can go back and look for it near that position at any other date or time (even at midday, if you have a telescope). Actually Polaris is not located precisely at the north celestial pole (point in the heavens situated exactly over Earth's north pole), so it does change its position slightly, tracing out a small circle during each 24-hour period. But this is still an immense advantage over most stars. If you find a typical star over a treetop at a certain part of twilight, it will not quite be there even the very next night; it will have risen about 4 minutes earlier (due to Earth's orbital motion) and thus have advanced farther across the sky. (By the way, do not forget that the time when twilight occurs also changes each night—though minimally at the equator and around the solstices.)

Questions

1. Can your naked eye see zero magnitude stars with the Sun just below or even just above the horizon?

2. How soon after sunset (or before sunrise) can stars of each magnitude first (or last) be glimpsed with the naked eye? At what point in dusk or dawn can you first or last see naked-eye deep-sky objects like the Pleiades or Andromeda Galaxy? or Polaris?

SUNSETS AND TWILIGHTS

46.

Color and Color Gradation of the Setting Sun

Watch as many sunsets (and sunrises) as possible, noting the change in color and gradation of color from top to bottom of the Sun when it is low in the sky. Compare the extent of reddening and gradation at different angular altitudes in the same sunset and at the same altitudes in different sunsets, learning how these factors correlate with various other sky and weather conditions.

The general explanations for the flattening (see the next activity) and the redness of the low sun are well known. The greater thickness of atmosphere (longer path through atmosphere) down low scatters out more of the rays of colors other than orange and red (because the other colors are of shorter wavelength). That thickness also refracts upward the rays from the bottom of the Sun (shining lower in the atmosphere) more strongly than those from the top of the Sun—causing the image to appear compressed in the vertical direction.

Yes, the general explanations for these low-sky effects are well understood. What is not understood, however, is just how strongly the effects are intensified (or diminished) by specific weather and sky conditions.

Needless to say, weather statistics on visibility (measured by the limiting distance at which things can be observed in the landscape) and humidity are relevant to the question of how reddened the low Sun will appear and what kind of particles or aerosols are contributing most to the reddening. It is also interesting to rate the blueness of the sky (see Activities 56 and 57) and the size of the Sun's aureole (see Activity 57) in conjunction with your rating of the low Sun's redness. And when should that rating be performed? At a number of different altitudes of the Sun, of course. Note how rapidly the reddening increases as a function of decreasing altitude of the Sun at different sunsets. Note how the Sun one day appears as red at 10 degrees above the horizon as it does another day at 1 degree.

At first your rating of the Sun's redness will be imprecise and too much affected by subjective factors. After a little practice, however, you can get good at rating each orange or red you see on an absolute scale. It is exciting to quest for the least red and most red sunsets you have ever seen and then to find what their corresponding meteorological and atmospheric conditions are. An important word of warning is needed, however: Your observations should not even begin until the Sun is extremely dimmed. If your eye is even slightly dazzled by the light, *don't look.* No sky sight, however beautiful or striking, is worth losing your vision for.

That includes the lovely sight of a Sun with several distinctly different colors grading one into the other up it. The top of the Sun may still look yellow when the middle is orange and the bottom is red. Of course, usually it is different shades of the same color that are noticed—the farther toward the red end of the spectrum, the lower on the solar disk. Take notes on how gradual or abrupt the transitions are, how many distinctly different shades you perceive, and how great a total difference there is from the hue at the top to the one at the bottom. Then seek to explain your observations by reference to weather information. The most extreme cases of numerous shades and abrupt gradations must result from distinct layering in the atmosphere.

Questions

1. How red is today's setting Sun at various altitudes in the sky? What is the altitude at which it is first noticeably red at a glance? (*Be careful you don't hurt your eyes!*) Do you find that sunsets are often redder than sunrises?

2. What are the visibility, humidity, sky blueness, and other conditions associated with different amounts of reddening in the low Sun? What amounts of which substances—water vapor, smoke particles, dust, volcanic ash or aerosol, and so on—produce given degrees of reddening?

3. What is the highest red Sun you can see on a cloudless (but hazy or smoky) day? What is the lowest yellow or white Sun on a very clear day? What are the precise atmospheric conditions at these times?

4. What atmospheric conditions can you connect with instances of strong or numerous gradations of color on the low Sun?

47.

Oblateness of the Setting Sun

Observe the Sun at different low angular altitudes and at different sunsets and sunrises, as in the previous activity. This time, however, note how flattened the Sun seems to you and also—by measuring the Sun's image on photos you take—how flattened it really appears. Keep track of weather and sky conditions in the hope of correlating them with different amounts of flattening at different sunsets.

Measuring how flattened the Sun appears at various sunsets and sunrises poses some difficulty. For a viewer at sea level, the average value of the Sun's flattening in the vertical dimension—its *oblateness*—is about 20 percent when the Sun is right on the horizon. In other words, the vertical dimension appears about 20 percent shorter than the horizontal. An observer in a jet airplane sees about twice as much flattening, but even he or she may not be able to detect, from his or her vantage point, the 7 percent flattening that the Sun has when it is still 5 degrees above the horizon. As a matter of fact, we are so used to seeing a flattened Sun near sunset or sunrise that we may find a 10 or 15 percent oblateness hard to notice. This can be overcome by looking at the Sun with your head tilted all the way to the side so that the horizontal dimension now seems vertical. But how can you measure the usually slight differences in flattening from night to night of so small an object (easily hideable by a dime at arm's length)—one that you cannot put on your table to get a ruler on?

You can get a ruler on the Sun if you take photographs. Of course, this will involve a little expense, but only for photos that anyone who likes even merely "pretty" pictures would approve. Most people already have a camera of some kind. A 35-millimeter camera is not strictly necessary for this particular activity. What is necessary, however, is to enlarge your apparent image a bit for measuring if you do not have a telephoto lens. Have an enlargement made of your print, or project your slide on a wall. Then measure the vertical and horizontal dimensions of the Sun's image, determining the ratio between them. Naturally, you should also measure on the print or the projected slide the exact altitude of the Sun above the horizon (very important since flattening changes with angular altitude). That is easy if you remember that the Sun is about 0.5 degree wide in its unaltered, horizontal dimension.

A final question: Why would the Sun's flattening vary on different nights? The answer is that the amount of refraction low in the sky varies from night to night—for reasons explained in the following activity.

Questions

1. How often does the flattening of the Sun on the horizon vary measurably (on your photographs) from its average of 20 percent flattening?

2. How do your measured values for the Sun's flattening on your photos at a certain sunset compare with your original rating of how strong the flattening seemed to you? What in the landscape or skyscape might account for your overestimating or underestimating the flattening sometimes?

3. What are the air and water temperatures associated with instances of extreme flattening? (See the next activity.)

48.

Distorted Sunsets

Examine the apparent shape of the Sun at every sunset (and sunrise) you can, looking for distortions and recording their frequency. Study (and sketch or photograph) each kind of distortion in detail as it progresses. Also try to obtain air and water temperatures and other weather information for your site and the area you watch the Sun over.

When the Sun sinks close to the horizon, it may shine in succession through layers of air with different temperatures and therefore different densities—causing a variety of distortions in the Sun's shape.

How do layers of different air density create misshapen Suns? These layers exist when there are unusually strong variations in temperature with height in the lowest part of the atmosphere. The colder air is, the denser; and therefore light rays tend to be refracted toward cooler air. But it is only when temperature varies drastically with height that very strong refraction results, and extreme distortions of the Sun's shape appear. Let us consider what happens in each of the cases in Figure 9—each of the cases you can look forward to observing and studying.

Example A, an even more flattened setting Sun than usual, will be produced when the normal greater refraction near the horizon is further increased by a layer of cold air not far above the warmer surface air. The cause of the narrow layer of warmer surface air is often a large body of water being warmer than the air well above it. (Only the narrow air layer near the water shares much of the water's heat.)

Example B shows an even more drastic case of the above scenario resulting in a mirage over water called the *countersun*. A perfect (except upside-down!) image of the Sun rises to meet the true Sun as the latter sets. The two then appear to touch and present a form more or less like that depicted in the illustration, before merging into each other further as the whole strange mass sets. There are less extreme instances, but there are also more extreme ones; I have seen the countersun get about half-risen before making contact with the true Sun! What is the countersun? It is the reflected image of the Sun on water which appears to rise above the horizon when all the light rays coming to the observer from the true horizon have been refracted up far enough to pass over the observer's head and not be seen at all. With the strip of your field of vision containing the horizon being removed, the reflected Sun can seem to meet the true Sun and melt into it.

Example C occurs in the opposite situation: Now we have warm air moving in over a much colder body of water, ice, or snow. In this case, certain light rays are refracted *down* out of our sight by the colder air. A whole strip of sky beneath the setting Sun becomes a *blind strip*. The result is that, when the Sun reaches the blind strip, it seems to set in thin air before it reaches the horizon. Only if you observe on

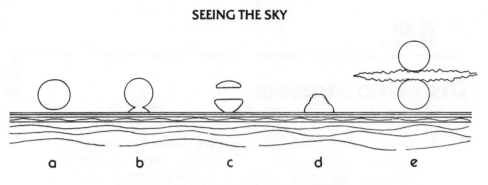

Figure 9 Various kinds of distorted sunsets.

a hill or other elevation will you get to see part of the Sun reappear below the blind strip, as in the illustration.

Example D shows what happens when there are several very narrow layers of strong temperature discontinuity. A horizontal bar or band from the Sun's disk can be refracted up and, being a wider part of the disk, stick out from either side of the upper Sun as one or more pairs of spikes. This is the *Chinese lantern sun*. As the Sun sinks through each discontinuity, an attendant bar may seem to move up the Sun's disk, detach, then contract and vanish—sometimes producing one version of the wondrous green flash. (See the next activity.)

Example E should not be confused with the previous fairly well understood sunset phenomena, all resulting from refraction by air. This strange sight, the double sun, is probably a halo phenomenon and is discussed in Activity 80 along with sun pillars.

Questions

1. How frequently do each of the kinds of distorted sunsets occur at your observing site? What variations in them do you notice? What is the farthest up you see the countersun get?

2. Do the air and water temperature readings you measure (and get from local weather reports) at these sunsets seem consistent with the above explanations of the distortions? What are the greatest differences in water and air temperatures (either air warmer or water warmer) you record? Do they correspond with the most extreme distortions of sunsets?

49.

The Green Flash

Look for the green segment and green flash at sunsets and sunrises, noting all particulars of what you see and all relevant sky and weather conditions.

On days that are not too hazy, a small amount of the blue and green light of the Sun manages to avoid being scattered or (unlike the yellow and orange) absorbed in its long pathway from the setting Sun to the observer. Of course, the red light still predominates in the image of the Sun reaching the observer. The tiny blue-green component would never be visible, were it not for a further factor. That factor is refraction, strong in the greater thickness of atmosphere down low but—and this is the key point—stronger for blue and green than for red. The image of the Sun in blue-green light is refracted (bent) up to very slightly higher in the sky than the image of the Sun in red light. The top of the blue-green component sticks up a bit farther than the top of the red one. And because it does, we can occasionally see the setting sun's last piece shine out green (or, much more rarely, blue) in what is called the *green flash.*

The green flash (also called the *green ray*) has a reputation for being rarely seen, and in some locales this is deserved—if one is looking for only the strong, truly flashlike version of the phenomenon. On the other hand, less dramatic versions of the effect must be far more common. Amid the confused terminology, I have long chosen to follow my interpretation of M. Minnaert's discussion (in his *The Nature of Light and Color in the Open Air*) and speak of the less dramatic instances as the *green rim* and the *green segment*. The green rim is a slight tingeing of the Sun's very upper edge, visible only with optical aid. But the green segment, visible to the naked eye, is seen as green tingeing of the extremities of the partly set Sun, which then spreads briefly across the remaining piece as the Sun disappears. Apparently this segment is one in which the green only predominates. The green flash itself (or green flash proper) is when a tiny, all-green tip of the Sun's top is seen entirely on its own for a second or so—appearing so small that the naked eye can not resolve it and sees it instead as a sudden, bright, green "star" flaring out.

This, at any rate, is a scheme for beginning to organize the observations of green light in the setting or rising Sun. Spectacular multiple green flashes and what seem truly raylike vertical extensions of green are also seen sometimes—yet more dramatic versions of this phenomenon. If you can observe several different versions of the green flash a number of times in the course of a season or a year of devoted sunset watching, see if your observations can be made to fit to this scheme—or to a better one of your own devising.

Above all else, try to gather as much precise information as you can about the weather conditions, and record as much as you can about the sky conditions (how red the Sun was on the horizon, how low it was before turning red, how blue the sky was). Too much humidity (water vapor) scatters out the remaining blue-green light. Presumably the most spectacular instances of the green flash occur when there is especially strong refraction—produced by large differences in temperature in the layers of air nearest to the horizon. These may be more likely between air and water, but looking over water is not essential (neither is having an extremely distant horizon, though it helps). Record water temperature and air temperature (the latter at several levels of the atmosphere if you can get this weather data) around the times you attempt to witness the green flash. (We want to know more about why it is not visible on some seemingly favorable occasions.)

By the way, the green flash can be observed at least as prominently at sunrise—but only if you know exactly where to look to catch the first piece of the Sun appearing. And the *blue* (or even violet!) *flash* results only when air is most extremely clear.

Questions

1. How often can you see the green segment and the green flash itself? What are the duration, the shade of green, and the other particulars?

2. What are the humidity and sky conditions (as measured by blueness of sky and so on) and the temperatures at various altitudes in the atmosphere when you see the green flash? When you do not see it?

50.

Crepuscular and Anticrepuscular Rays

Look for and note the position of crepuscular rays and anticrepuscular rays after sunset or before sunrise. Then try identifying them with cloudy areas on the TV weather satellite photos.

Crepuscular means "of twilight," and *crepuscular rays* are strips of blue-gray shadow radiating out from the Sun's position below the horizon during twilight. In broad daylight we may see what we call sunbeams separated by long shadows of parts of clouds. But crepuscular rays are the shadows of clouds or cloud masses that are typically several hundred miles away, below our horizon; so these shadows are vastly long and often seen together in a sometimes sky-spanning fan among the lovely tints and mysterious glows of twilight.

You should always trace out a crepuscular ray as far as possible across the sky. If it is lost from view high in the heavens of dusk, carry on your gaze to see if it is resumed in the east by an *anticrepuscular ray* converging on a spot exactly opposite the Sun's (below-the-horizon) position. This actually is the same cloud shadow, as proven by the fact that crepuscular ray and anticrepuscular ray are sometimes seen to meet—one beam across the entire sky.

Usually the rays are not seen to stretch so far, because high in the sky we are looking through the shortest path of atmosphere, with the least total amount of particles that can scatter to us the twilight glow against which the crepuscular ray stands out. Activities 53 through 55 discuss twilight glows in detail. But I must note here that the particles must be the high ones from volcanic eruptions (always present, to some extent, 7 and more miles up, even when there have been no major eruptions in the world recently). The visibility of crepuscular rays ought not to be aided by dust or water vapor lower in the atmosphere, though a certain amount of high cirrus clouds can play the role of the thin volcanic ash or aerosols in aiding the visibility of twilight glow and therefore crepuscular rays.

Today's widespread availability of weather satellite photos on TV means the average person can often easily check on the location of clouds that were causing the crepuscular rays he or she saw. How heavy is the cloud mass producing the rays? Is it an area of heavy thunderstorm or lighter cloud? With this final piece of information and with your knowledge of twilight glows gained from the twilight glow activities, you may be able to ferret out how much each factor contributes to the visibility of crepuscular rays: strong twilight glow (from volcanic particles or cirrus clouds); clear lower atmosphere; and deep intrinsic darkness of cloud shadow (due to the heaviness of the cloud producing it).

Questions

1. How often can you observe crepuscular rays? Anticrepuscular rays? The two joined to form one sky-spanning beam? What is the greatest number of the rays you ever observe?

2. On TV satellite weather photographs, can you identify which cloud mass was producing a given crepuscular ray you observed in a certain (cardinal) direction?

3. Can you identify how much of a role clear lower atmosphere, strong twilight glow, and heavy shadow-producing cloud each play in the prominence of a certain display of crepuscular rays?

51.

The Earthshadow and Belt of Venus

Look for the earthshadow and the Belt of Venus in the east after sunset (or in the west before sunrise). Determine to how high an angular altitude each rises in dusk before being lost from view or (in the earth shadow's case) having its edge become indistinct. Rate the initial prominence of these features, too. Finally, check two things—the clearness of the atmosphere at your location and the clearness (or lack of clearness) at the "tangent point" many miles to your west—and test how these things are related to the visibility of the earthshadow and Belt of Venus.

Not many people realize that the shadow of Earth can often be seen projected in the east sky at dusk (or in the west sky at dawn). We see it in cross-section, appearing as a blue-grey segment thickest in the position opposite where the Sun went down. And sometimes— but not always—visible along the earthshadow's top edge is a lovely pink border, which has been called the *Belt of Venus*.

The earthshadow and Belt rise at first with the Sun's speed, eventually two to three times faster. If the Belt has been visible at all, it is the first to disappear, the distinction between blue sky and the deeper blue-gray of the earthshadow remaining visible—for a while.

The explanation for these phenomena's visibility and behavior is made evident in Figure 10. The tangent rays from Sun to *tangent point* on Earth (where an observer would be seeing sunset) continue on to define the boundary between sunlit atmosphere and earthshadowed atmosphere. It is these tangent rays (and those just above them) which, deeply reddened by their long trip through the atmosphere, are scattered back to us as the Belt of Venus. A moment's thought shows that, if clouds are blocking the sunset as seen from the tangent point (which moves at a great rate of speed westward away from the observer during twilight), the rays producing the Belt are not just reddened, but cut off. Of course, if bright sunlight is still flooding over the cloudtops at the tangent point, the earthshadow itself may remain prominent anyway. On nights when you see the earthshadow but not the Belt of Venus, or neither despite clear skies at your own location, check the weather satellite photos on TV to see where and what kind of cloudiness was west of you.

Figure 10 also helps us understand why the earthshadow's top rises ever more quickly and becomes indistinct as it gets higher in the sky. The apparent speed increases because the tangent line cuts an ever-steeper path through the atmosphere as seen by the observer. (The same geographical rate of advance is translated into an ever-faster angular advance.) The tangent line (the border

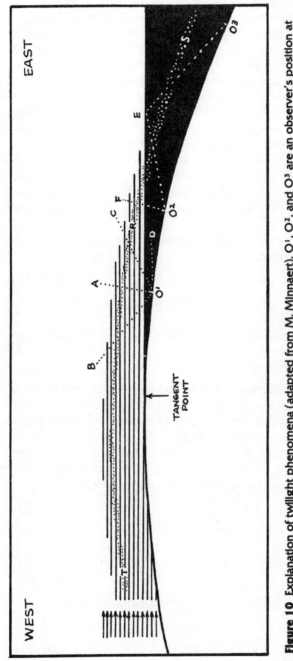

Figure 10 Explanation of twilight phenomena (adapted from M. Minnaert). O¹, O², and O³ are an observer's position at times increasingly late in evening twilight. A is at the zenith for O¹, B, midway up the west/west, and C, midway up the east/west. D is the boundary of the illuminated atmosphere, F is at the zenith for O². ST is a layer of volcanic ash or aerosol, R is the position of the upper edge of the Belt of Venus when it is visible for a while after sunset.

between sunlit and earthshadowed atmosphere) also passes through a shorter path of atmosphere east of the observer as the earthshadow gets higher; finally there is too little atmosphere along the path to scatter back enough light to make the distinction between shadowed and lit atmosphere discernible.

One expert, M. Minnaert, stresses that the earthshadow can be followed fairly far up into the eastern sky only if the observer's atmosphere is very clear. Another set of experts, Aden and Marjorie Meinel, stress that a strong haze layer in the atmosphere can increase the backscattering of light and render the earthshadow more prominent. The Meinels stress that the sunlight streaming through the atmosphere at the tangent point must also be bright to produce a good earthshadow—but since hazy skies are likely to occur over a fairly large geographical region, would not the same haze that enhanced the backscattering usually also dim the Sun? To help clarify this matter, take note of the blueness of your sky—and, by weather reports, the likely blueness (unhaziness) of the sky hundreds of miles west of you. Then see how these factors relate to the visibility of the earthshadow.

Do not mistake a pink border of clouds on the eastern horizon around sunset for the true Belt of Venus (which rises in cloudfree air).

Questions

1. How often can you see the earthshadow? The Belt of Venus? Can you relate the absence of either or both to cloudiness at the tangent point west of you? (Check TV weather satellite photos.)

2. To what angular altitude can you follow the Belt and the top edge of the earthshadow in their rise? Does how high they get correspond exactly with the initial prominence you rate them to have? How are these two properties—initial prominence and maximum altitude visible—affected by the amount of haze in the atmosphere (at the observer's site and, a little later, at the tangent point to the west)? Where should haze be and where should clear skies be to produce the most prominent and the highest visible earthshadow?

52.

Brightness of Twilight

As twilight progresses, measure the brightness of the twilight sky in various directions by readability of standard size print.

Activity 8 was, in part, a study of the brightness of the Moon at various phases. I suggested measuring the brightness by seeing what size print could be read—that is, read without truly straining your eyes. The same can be done with the brightness of twilight.

In this case we can turn our book or magazine in several different directions at each stage of twilight to test the illumination levels. (By the way, it is interesting to compare them to the power of moonlight determined by the Activity 8 tests.) If it is evening twilight we are studying, the illumination from the west will naturally be brightest. (But in the next activity, we will see that from exactly where in the west is quite surprising.) Which is next brightest—light from overhead or from the east? To test the former, be in a place where only the light from directly above comes down to your printed page.

How each direction's amount of illumination changes during twilight is a fascinating drama. Study the changes carefully, and see whether they are always the same changes from night to night. (To do this more accurately, you may need to use several different sizes of print.) You will also find that some twilights are brighter than others. (The explanation for this is found in our next activity.)

Using a standard size print (from a famous newspaper or magazine) has the advantage of simplified repeatability for the largest number of people possible. Nevertheless, you will find it interesting to study at what stage in twilight various objects (and details of objects) in your local landscape can no longer be seen from your observing site or from certain distances.

The attempt to determine when in twilight it becomes difficult to see certain things and perform certain activities has importance for society. The end of *civil twilight* is said to come when many such activities—especially driving a motor vehicle—become too difficult without artificial illumination. This civil twilight ends when the Sun is 6 degrees below the horizon; *nautical twilight* (when a sea horizon ceases to be visible), when the Sun is 12 degrees down; and *astronomical twilight* (last touch of glow gone from the west), when the Sun is 18 degrees down. Near the equinoxes at middle latitudes, these *solar depressions* occur about ½, 1, and 1½ hours after sunset, respectively. But at other times of year and other latitudes, the times can be very different. So always note the time, date, and latitude of your twilight observations.

Questions

1. Until how late in evening twilight can you read print of a standard size with your text illuminated from the west only? From the east only? From overhead only?
2. Using several standard sizes of print, how does the illumination coming from each of these directions vary during the course of twilight? How much from one twilight to another?

53.

The Purple Light

Look for the twilight glow called the purple light. *Note the times when it first appears, when it is most prominent, and when it is last visible. At each of these times (and others), measure its angular size or at least the angular altitude of the top of it. Record any color you see, also any pecularities of structure. Check a weather satellite photo, if possible, to see how far to your west (east, if morning twilight) skies are clear. If the purple light is strong, look for the other special phenomena of volcanically enhanced twilights. (See Activities 54 and 55.)*

When the Sun is a certain angular distance below the horizon, the strongest twilight is not coming from low in the west—it is coming from partway up the west sky! This radiance may bathe the west side of objects with an eerie light from on high and may glow purple or pink (though it is most often too weak to show much color). This giant patch of illumination in the sky is called the *purple light*.

The cause of the purple light is shown back in Figure 10. The light, appearing in direction B for an observer at 0_1, is that scattered to us from the second passage of sunlight through a layer of particles or aerosols (ST) in the atmosphere. (That a second passage occurs is merely due to the fact that the layer and atmosphere follow the curve of our round Earth.) The causative layer is typically located about 6 to 12 miles up. There can no longer be any doubt that its particles or aerosols are derived from volcanoes, even just the minor eruptions around the world being enough to keep the supply replenished. A major eruption can cause great enhancement of the purple light and produce other special effects. (See Activities 54 and 55.)

When no major eruption of the proper kind has occurred for several years (the usual situation), the purple light is generally weak and colorless. But you still may notice it as a subtly brighter area about 20 to 30 degrees above the west horizon when the Sun is about 3 to 6 degrees below the horizon (very roughly 15 to 30 minutes after sunset—remember the solar depression varies with latitude and time of year).

No purple light at all can form if there is much cloudiness at the *tangent point*. This tangent point is located very roughly about 300 miles in the direction of the departed Sun for an observer during the period when the purple light would typically be strongest. So when you see the light one night but not the next, check a TV weather satellite photo to see if cloudiness at that point may have been responsible for the purple light's absence.

Use your fist (about 10 degrees wide when held out at arm's length) to measure the angular altitude of the top of the purple light when it first appears, when it is strongest, and when it disappears. These angular altitudes can be used to compute the true altitudes of the material scattering the light—as long as you carefully record time, date, and latitude of your observation.

Keep track of the changes in the purple light's intensity from night to night and month to month. After seeing a few good displays, you may be able to start giving numerical ratings. You may have no spectacular shows of it for a long time. (Even on nonvolcanic nights, however, there can sometimes be a widespread network of cirrus clouds that will enhance and spread the purple light.) But when a volcano in some remote region on Earth erupts ash or gas that drifts over large areas of the planet, you may be one of the first to know!

Questions

1. Can you detect the purple light as at least a slight increase in illumination tonight? If not, might clouds at the tangent point be the reason? How often can you see the purple light?

2. How great (on a 0 to 10 scale) is the intensity of the purple light on various nights? Can you detect any trends of increasing or decreasing intensity over periods of weeks or over the year?

3. What is the angular altitude of the top of the purple light when it first appears? When it is strongest? When it disappears? At what times do these events occur?

4. If the purple light has extraordinarily vivid color, brightness, extent, or duration, do you know of any volcanic eruption in recent months that might be associated? (Check the *SEAN Bulletin;* see Suggested Reading List.)

54.

Various Phenomena of Volcanically Enhanced Twilights

Be on the lookout for any of the special phenomena of volcanic twilights (and volcanic daytime sky). If the purple light is unusually strong or enduring, perform the tasks of the previous activity with special attention. If ultra-cirrus clouds, Bishop's Ring, or very strong primary glow are observed, carefully describe and measure them. (See the next activity for the second purple light and counter purple light.)

In the 50 years after Mount Katmai's 1912 eruption, there were only fairly localized outbreaks of volcanic twilights featuring the special phenomena that are the object of this activity. But then there were more widespread, some even worldwide outbreaks for long periods in the early 1960s, 1970s, and, especially, 1980s. No one knows when the next major eruption to affect the world's atmosphere will occur, but when it does, you will want to be ready.

The first sign may be greatly enhanced purple light. (See Activity 53.) But sometimes it may be the appearance of intense *primary glow*. The purple light is a secondary glow in the sense of light being scattered to us from its second passage through the permanent layer of volcanic material (almost surely volcanic aerosols) 6 to 12 miles up. This is illustrated back in Figure 10. You can see in that diagram that the sunlight's primary (first) trip through the layer—and through any part of the atmosphere directly between us and the general direction of the Sun—would result in scattering causing a primary glow. When affected by an eruption, the primary glow band—really a segment, thickest above the departed sun's position—lies along the horizon in a strip, which is first yellow, then (minutes later) orange, then (more minutes later) red before it sets. When enhanced by a major eruption, its early stage may display it extending up to about 15 degrees; or it may even be visible earlier than early—that is, even before sunset.

If enough ash is carried (on high-altitude winds) over an observer's locale, the ash may be visible in the form of clouds after sunset (in extreme cases, even before sunset). Long, delicate, and gray (sometimes slightly ruddy), they have been called *ultra-cirrus clouds* because when ordinary cirrus have ceased to be sunlit, ultra-cirrus clouds (*ultra*—"beyond," here meaning "higher than") are still illuminated by the Sun. A typical height for them is about 7 miles, such that they only remain visible until the Sun is a few degrees below the horizon.

Many effects of volcanic twilights are produced not by ash but by a sulfuric-acid aerosol haze produced from vast release of sulfur-dioxide gas. Quite possibly, these tiny aerosol particles (but certainly volcanic ash) can cause a legendary phenomenon called *Bishop's Ring*. (The phenomenon is named after Reverend

Sereno Bishop, the first person—in 1883 after Krakatau—to describe it.) It is actually a corona (see Activity 85) of a special kind. It appears as a dimly silver-blue area of roughly 15 to 25 degrees (sometimes more) radius bounded by a wide, usually indistinct band of a slightly brownish or ruddy hue.

A final twilight change may be the appearance of the second purple light and counter purple light—the subjects of the next activity.

Questions

1. Do you recall ever having seen a great and enduring display of the purple light or primary glow? If you see either—or Bishop's Ring or ultra-cirrus clouds—this year, do you know what volcanic eruption the display may be associated with?

2. How long after sunset does the primary glow or the purple light set? (Or, if they disappear before setting, at what altitude and time?)

3. What is the angular radius of the silver-blue area in each Bishop's Ring display you see? What is the angular width of the brown or ruddy band? What is the angular altitude of ultra-cirrus clouds when you last see them illuminated (which is to say, when you last see them), and what time after sunset does this occur? What is the orientation of the clouds with respect to the horizon? (Which end is higher?)

55.

Second Purple Light and Counter Purple Light

In the rare seasons when the purple light is greatly enhanced by a major volcanic eruption, watch for the second purple light and the counter purple light. Carefully record the times when each of the three glows appears, is strongest, and disappears, measuring the angular height of their tops (and in the case of the counter purple light, its bottom)—especially at the time they are lost to view. Rate the intensities of each of them from night to night. When one (or more) of them is absent or weak, note on TV weather satellite photos whether cloudiness at the tangent point could explain this.

Following a major eruption that causes a high-altitude haze of sulfuric acid aerosols over parts of the world, observers may eventually begin to see the *second purple light*.

After the usually pinkish first purple light sinks and dwindles, a large and generally more purple area of radiance may appear roughly where the first one did. The Sun may be 6 to 8 degrees below the horizon. In the most extreme cases, second purple light may not set until the end of astronomical twilight—the Sun 18 degress below the horizon, at least one-and-one-half hours after sunset!

The mystery of the second purple light is whether it is really caused by volcanic aerosols sometimes as high as 50 or more miles altitude or whether it is caused by the illumination of the first purple light on aerosols at a much lower altitude (the same altitude as those that caused the first purple light). The latter theory thus is suggesting that the second purple light is a kind of twilight of twilight!

To help decide between these theories, you should not only measure the angular height of the top of both purple lights when they are last seen (recording the times carefully), but also rate the intensity of each. Rate each separately on its own 0 to 10 scale of intensity. (The first light is brighter than the second in absolute terms, but the second can seem as prominent because it is in a later, darker sky.)

You can also check the evening's TV weather satellite photos to see how the two purple lights are affected by cloudiness or clearness at the appropriate tangent points. (See Activities 51 and 53 and Figure 10 for explanation of the tangent point.) A twilight glow that set about 40 minutes after the Sun and was caused directly by the Sun would have a tangent point about 450 to 650 miles away from the observer. A twilight glow that set 70 minutes after the Sun, however, could have a tangent point as much as 1,000 or more miles away.

Solving the mystery of the second purple light might be aided by observations of what I call the *counter purple light*. It is only visible, I think, when volcanic aerosols are plentiful enough to cause the second purple light. When the counter purple light is seen, it is a purple or reddish purple glow low in the east during evening twilight, usualy prominent after the first purple light starts fading and before the second purple light brightens. There is no doubt that it rises, with its lower edge being the more discernible. It is this lower edge whose angular altitude one should measure—especially at the time (carefully noted) that it is last visible. Is counter purple light simply radiance backscattered to us from aerosols in the east being lit by the first purple light? If so, then why does it not appear earlier? Perhaps it is actually caused by the second purple light!

Be sure to note the colors of each of these purple light glows. It has been assumed that the purple color is a mixture of reddened sunlight with a little sky blue still left. But if so, then why are the second and counter lights usually far more purple than the first one? Part of the answer may be that the eye becomes preferentially more sensitive to the blue-violet end of the spectrum as light levels dim.

Questions

1. Do you recall having seen the second purple light or counter purple light in 1982 or 1983, after the El Chichón eruptions? If you see them this year, what times do they first appear, shine strongest, and disappear? What is the angular

altitude of their tops (and, in the counter purple light's case, its bottom), especially when they set or are last visible?

2. What are the intensities (each on its own 0 to 10 scale) of the purple light, the second purple light, and the counter purple light on various nights? If, some nights, one or more is absent, do TV weather satellite photos indicate that the reason is cloudiness at the tangent points? Exactly what is the color of each of the glows each night?

THE BLUE SKY

56.

Blueness (and Darkness) of the Blue Sky

Observe and rate the deepness of blue in the darkest (most deeply blue) part of the sky from day to day, always with the Sun at the same angular altitude. Observe how the blueness changes with changing solar altitude, independent of changes in the humidity. Use either your impressions or an extremely inexpensive cyanometer for rating.

One of the simplest yet greatest beauties of the heavens is the blue sky. It is air molecules themselves that scatter the blue from out of white (or yellow-white) sunlight. What makes a cloudless sky (or area of sky) less blue on some days than on others is mostly the presence of greater amounts of water vapor. Of course, dust and pollen and, in some places, manmade air pollutants can also play a role in lessening the blue: That is to say, these particles scatter all wavelengths—not just blue—so that a white light is scattered from them and rivals or even overwhelms the blue component in the color of the sky.

A person can study the color of each day's sky and after a while be able to assign a numerical rating on a scale from brightest white to darkest blue (the deeper the shade of blue, the darker the sky). A great help in training the eye to this, however, is a *cyanometer*—nothing more than a scale of hues made by mixing certain proportions of blue paint and white paint on a piece of cardboard or on strips of cardboard!

When you use your cyanometer you should have the same light source on your painted colors as the sky does—full sunlight—behind you and thus shining directly on your colors. You should also do your day-to-day ratings with the Sun at the same angular altitude because the degree of blueness in the bluest spot will change with changing Sun altitude.

The reason is made clear by consideration of the question, where is the deepest blue in the sky? Since you may not always have an unobstructed view of the entire sky to make sure for yourself, it is good to know a rule that determines where the spot will be, anyway.

There are three factors that affect what will be the location of the bluest spot in the sky, and all are dependent on the Sun's position. The factors are, (1) how near in the sky to the Sun a point is (close to the Sun, scattering is very strong, especially by the larger particles in air that forward-scatter much more than they do in other directions); (2) how near to 90 degrees away from the Sun a spot is (this is the angle at which there is the least scattering of light); and (3) how low in the sky a spot is (the lower you gaze, the longer a pathway containing dust and water vapor you are looking through). If you combine all these factors, you come up with the following rule: The bluest, darkest spot in the sky generally lies on a vertical circle passing through the Sun at a point about 95 degrees from the Sun when the Sun is low and at a point about 65 degrees from the Sun when it is high.

Questions

1. What is your rating for the darkest part of the sky today? At different times during the day?

2. How much does your rating change from day to day? How well does it correlate with the relative humidity? After many dry days, can you note an effect, in addition to humidity, presumably resulting from more dust in the air?

3. What is the bluest rating you ever give to a day's bluest sky?

57.

Distribution of Blue in the Sky and the Sun's Aureole

Using the knowledge (and perhaps the cyanometer) from the previous activity, rate the distribution of blueness (and thus of brightness, or lack of) over the entire sky at various times of day and on various days. Being careful to block the Sun from view and not look too long, try to determine the angular size of the "aureole."

The previous activity stated the three factors that affect the location of the bluest point in the sky and a simple rule that was the result of all the factors. The blueness—relative to the rest of the sky—of any point in the sky at any time could be roughly predicted in the same way. But that is no replacement for actual observation of the distribution of light in the blue sky.

M. Minnaert advises the use of a small mirror to compare one section of the sky to another, but his key advice is to let your eyes map the lines—or at least areas—of equal brightness (that is, equal blueness) around the heavens. These *isophotes* or *isocyans* can be drawn on a diagram of the kind shown in Figure 11.

The overall pattern is found to be a bright area surrounding the Sun and another bright area opposite, separated by a "line of darkness," which runs through the darkest point in the sky. But there are far more details to be noted. On the very clearest days, there is a beautiful compression of many shades of blue into

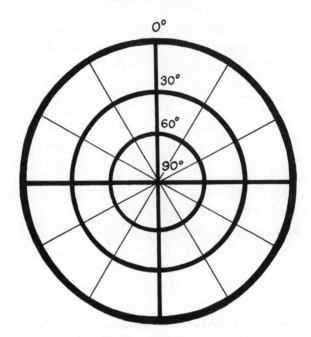

Figure 11 Chart of sky for blue-sky observations (figures in degrees are angular altitude in sky).

a relatively small range of altitudes down near the horizon. A vast region of sky around the Sun is of special interest and dramatic changeability. (It would be interesting to combine this activity with Activity 18 and find out how blue an area of sky must be before your naked eye can detect Venus in it—both when Venus is dimmest and when Venus is brightest.) The innermost area of hue discrete from others around the Sun is often called the *aureole*.

One measure of the clearness of the sky is the radius of this entirely white, brightest area. Actually, if there is at least a tinge of blue visible right up to the disk of the Sun (be careful of your eyes), then some experts would call this the Sun without any aureole at all. This is a situation well worth watching for, because, in most climates, it is quite rare—an indication of an exceedingly clear sky.

Questions

1. What do your diagrams of the distribution of light in the blue sky typically show? Just what changes are related to what levels of humidity, and can you distinguish these changes from those caused by dust and particulate matter in the air?

2. What is the size of the Sun's aureole today, and how does it vary during the day? From day to day and season to season? How often is it absent—blue visible right to the Sun's disk—and what other sky and weather conditions occur at those times?

LIGHT POLLUTION

58.

Mapping Light Pollution Areas
and Identifying City Skyglows

*At suburban or rural observing sites, locate manmade skyglows and identify
which cities produce each. Note roughly the size and severity of each glow.
Then use a map to measure distances from the cities to your site, and employ
Walker's Law to determine which cities produce an average amount of
skyglow for their populations and which produce more and less than average.*

Light pollution is that component of manmade outdoor lighting that is wasted
through being either excessive or misdirected. Unfortunately, few cities have yet
enacted the reforms they could to limit light pollution. As a result, light pollution is
costing many cities millions of dollars a year (per city!)—and degrading even rural
observers' view of the stars and other celestial beauties.

The key to getting political action against light pollution is educating the
public and the political officials. And a big step toward doing that is to gather data
about light pollution in your own area—such as you can accomplish in this activity
and in the following ones. If you learn exactly how bad light pollution is at various
sites, this will also help you choose the best sites possible until light pollution is
lessened.

The first step is to go to a suburban or rural site you would observe from and
to locate the different areas of "skyglow" around the horizon. Although such glows
may be most striking when there are low or medium altitude clouds over the cities,
it is most appropriate to go out on a cloudfree night of average sky transparency.

If you had not looked carefully before, you may not have realized that small
glows were visible from cities dozens of miles away. But as you check distance and
population of cities in your road atlas, you might also be surprised that the
closeness of a city is proportionally much more important than its size (that is, its
population). As a matter of fact, it turns out that the same source at half the distance
has six times the effect. Put another way, a city of 30,000 people 10 miles away has as
much effect as a city of 180,000 people 20 miles away!

These results can be predicted by a formula known as *Walker's Law*. (See
Table 9.) Of course, it is not population alone but the amount of illumination per
capita that really counts. Walker's Law predicts well for cities in which the average
lumens (units of illumination) per person is between 500 and 1,000. But large cities
tend to put out more light per person. There are also cities that are extra wasteful.
By seeing if a glow at your observing site looks more prominent than it should
according to Walker's Law, you can identify those cities that have a special problem
with light pollution. (If they are informed in the proper manner, city officials

Table 9
**Light pollution from cities as a function of population
and distance**

Distance at which significant observing degradation is beginning (sky glow 10 percent above natural background halfway up sky in the city's direction); can be matched with population of a city that would cause such degradation:

Distance (kilometers/miles)	Population
10/6.2	3,160
25/16.5	31,250
50/31	177,000
100/62	1,000,000
200/124	5,600,000

Effect of distance on the fall-off of sky glow (relative to "1" at 100 kilometers):

Distance (kilometers/miles)	Light Level
10/6.2	316
20/12.4	56
30/18.6	20
40/24.8	10
50/31	6
60/37.2	4
80/49.6	2
100/62	1

Data from Dr. David Crawford; calculated from Walker's Law

($I = 0.001 \times$ population $\times\, r^{-2.5}$, where I is increase in sky brightness——0.2 would mean a 20% increase above the 0.0 natural sky brightness—and r is distance in kilometers.)

should be interested to know that they have a problem whose correction could save residents a lot of money!)

Questions

1. How many separate regions of city skyglow can you identify from your suburban or rural observing site? Which city or metropolitan area is producing each glow?

2. How well does the prominence of each glow conform with the prediction of Walker's Law? Are any cities worse than predicted?

3. By using your observations and Walker's Law, can you find a much better site for astronomy within fairly easy driving distance?

117

59.

Severity of Light Pollution

Perform a more detailed study of how light pollution affects the sky at your site (and other sites) by measuring the angular size of the glows and checking the limiting magnitude of stars within them and elsewhere in the sky.

One of the prime goals of Activity 57 was to discern lines or areas of equal brightness (isophotes) in the blue sky of day and plot them on a chart or diagram like that of Figure 11. For many of us, surrounded on all sides by city skyglows, doing the same for the night sky would not be much more difficult. We would find that size and intensity of the city skyglows also does change in accordance with changes in humidity and air pollution—and with time of night, since there are less lights on late at night.

But if we took moonless nights of average transparency and went out at the same time on all of them, we should find the distribution of skyglow from cities similar from night to night. Consequently, after plotting a skyglow map this month on such a night (or on a few such to check our results), we could, next season and next year, perform the same task and be able to show how much worse skyglows had gotten—impressive data to give to cities you want to have reduce their light pollution.

Of course, one can do better than rating the brightness of parts of the night sky on a scale of values that are merely relative to each other. At certain important points in the sky, one can find the limiting magnitude of stars.

For finding the effect on limiting magnitudes of city skyglow alone, it is obviously best to pick a night when there is not an extra variable like the presence of haze. And you will have to refer to Table 3 for atmospheric extinction values at various altitudes in the sky.

Unfortunately, light pollution has some effect even on the sky well beyond what you perceive as a skyglow. Is the limiting magnitude at your zenith or at an area of sky as far as possible from any skyglow? Is even this poorer than it naturally would be? Probably. Drive to a farther site until there is no longer effect on the zenith limiting magnitude. How far did you have to go—if you made it at all?

By the way, this activity and the previous activity are most appropriate from a rural, a suburban or, at least, a small-city site. If you live in a larger city (and observe there), the next activity is better for you.

Questions

1. At various sites: How large in angular measure are the skyglows you perceive? What is the distribution of brightness from skyglow that you find in your plotting

of isophotes on a diagram of the sky? How does the distribution change during the night? How does it change after a season or a year?

2. At various sites: What is the limiting magnitude of stars in various parts of the skyglows? at the zenith? in the least affected sky?

60.

Identifying Local Sources of Skyglow

Identify individual sources of skyglow and light pollution in nearby cities, especially your own city, if you live in one. Make notes of what kind of lighting and shielding is used by these sources.

Even if you do not live in a city or do not observe the heavens from one, you almost certainly have a city's glow on your horizon and are ultimately threatened by a worsening of light pollution from it. Therefore all of us should study what parts of the sky are brightest from various spots in our home city or in cities nearest us. By doing so, we can track down which sections of an urban (or suburban) area are emitting the most skyglow and seek the specific offending sources.

What are the specific sources of skyglow? A street so overlit people can read fine print in their cars? A car dealership with lights that glare right out into passing drivers' eyes? Lights with no shielding whatsoever, so that more of their light is wasted than serves any useful purpose? You may find all of these, but before you discuss them—courteously but resolutely—with local government officials, you should learn the basics about different kinds of lighting and shielding.

Figure 12 illustrates different kinds of shielding and identifies which are most and least wasteful. A small shopping plaza using unshielded lights may be more of a skyglow culprit than a much larger shopping mall with full cutoff shielding. Find examples of good outdoor lighting in your area, too, so that people are assured you are not entirely negative or asking for the impossible. Convince people that what you want is quality lighting that suits its task and does not misdirect or otherwise waste illumination and energy.

The other aspect of lighting to identify—partly with help from seeing its skyglow from far away—is the kind of light used. Incandescent lights are the oldest kind, with their familiar light bulbs, but they are becoming quite rare in outdoor lighting because they are the least cost-effective variety. Other common outdoor

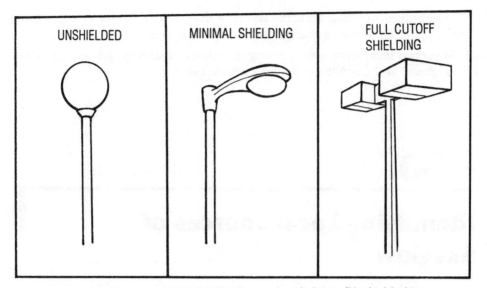

Figure 12 Different kinds of shielding for outdoor lighting. (Unshielded is most wasteful; full cutoff is least wasteful.)

lights are emission types. Mercury vapor lights emit a radiance that seems mostly whitish. But they too are now being replaced by sodium lights—high-pressure sodium (HPS) and low-pressure sodium (LPS).

Immensely the more common of the two is yellow HPS (though for several reasons, most city skyglows look pink from a distance). LPS shines with a deep golden light and is the most cost-effective of all. Professional astronomers especially like LPS because it is nearly *monochromatic*—its light is almost all of the same color; and, since that means a single wavelength, LPS can be filtered out to leave most of the light from astronomical objects undisturbed. On the other hand, LPS being monochromatic also means it renders the colors of objects poorly, which can be a severe drawback in certain situations. The solution is to use LPS with other lighting in such situations. But for many applications, LPS, even used alone, is the best: Its wavelength is near that at which the eye is most sensitive, so it permits the greatest visibility. (This is excellent for indoor security lighting, highways, and—as the U.S. Navy has found—the flight decks of aircraft carriers.)

If you find mostly HPS (maybe mercury vapor) lighting in your city, you should help promote LPS. (Try to find places in your area where LPS is used, and document that it has served its purpose well.) Of course, even LPS will not save a lot of money or lessen skyglow if it is not shielded or is used at greater lighting levels than are needed.

Using skyglows as your clues in this activity, you can track down the most and least wastefully lit parts of cities and speak intelligently to city officials who can enact reforms. (For information on all these matters—including how to approach a local government and how to initiate ordinances to limit light pollution (these have worked in many cities)—write to the International Dark-sky Association, 3545 N. Stewart, Tucson, AZ 85716.)

Questions

1. Which sections of the city you live in or live near produce the most skyglow? What are the specific sources of it?

2. Are the sources guilty of using poorly shielded lights, or too much light for the task? Are their lights incandescent, mercury vapor, HPS, LPS, or other? Would LPS, or a predominance of LPS, be better for that lighting task?

61.

Calculating Constellations Lost

On a clear, moonless evening, see what your limiting magnitude for stars is at several different altitudes in the sky north, south, and overhead. Then, using these figures and a star atlas plus Table 11, figure out how many constellations you have lost from the ranks of those visible in a naturally dark sky. Perform the same observations and calculations for different sites.

Our purpose will be to get a rough estimate of how many constellations are rendered invisible to the naked eye by light pollution at a given observing site. To simplify matters, I will give a plan for observers living near 40 degrees north latitude. This could be fairly easily adapted by viewers at significantly different latitudes.

Table 10 defines categories of constellations that reach a certain maximum altitude in the sky, and then, for viewers at 40 degrees north latitude, the declination range of constellations that would fit those categories. (The declination range would be different at other latitudes, and you would want to take into account the larger or smaller area of circumpolar constellations, so a few of your altitude categories might be different, too.)

On a typical, clear, moonless night, go out and find the limiting magnitude of stars—at 15, 30, 45, and 60 degrees high in the north sky; at the zenith; and at 60 and 40 degrees high in the north sky. Then take the mean between each limiting magnitude and its successor at the next observation altitude, and assign it to the appropriate altitude class or category. This is not difficult: If your limiting magnitude was 3.0 at 30 degrees high in the south and 4.0 at 45 degrees high in the south, then category 2 has a magnitude halfway between the two figures—3.5. (By the way, notice we are ignoring—as too dimmed by lowness for our purposes here, but not for those of Activity 41—those stars between +35 and −50 degrees declination for observers at 40 degrees north latitude. There is no category for stars below 40 degrees high in the north sky because all these circumpolar stars eventually will swing round to 40 degrees or more altitude.)

After you have obtained your (admittedly approximate) magnitude figures for each category, you are ready to check out a star atlas (or any set of star maps showing stars down through at least magnitude 5). Note the declination of each constellation, and see in which category it should be placed. Now all you have to do is find how many stars are fainter than your limiting magnitude figure for that category.

If no star in the constellation is as bright as the limiting magnitude, then you have completely lost this constellation from your naked-eye vision. But consider how many stars it takes to make a constellation a constellation. The essential outlines of many constellations are built up of numerous stars. But if we were forced to choose a minimum number—we might say three—any constellation in which we cannot observe at least three stars with the naked eye is essentially lost to us. (About the only outstanding exception to this I can think of is Canis Minor, whose essential form is depicted with just two stars.)

The constellations offer not just a helpful way of organizing areas of the heavens but also hundreds and even thousands of years of lore and other connections to our cultures and our hearts. Tell people what they are missing— especially in severely light-polluted areas for which you do this activity. Do they know their Zodiac constellations (even if only for silly astrological reasons)? Tell them how much of that Zodiac (some of it by faintness particularly susceptible to light pollution) has vanished from their sky.

Table 10
Declination ranges for altitude classes, at 40 degrees north latitude

Category	Altitude	Declination Range
1	15-30 south	−35 to −20
2	30-45 south	−20 to −5
3	45-60 south	−5 to +10
4	60-90 south	+10 to +40
5	90-60 north	+40 to +70
6	60-40 north	+70 to +90

Altitude figures are in degrees, and *north* and *south* mean north sky and south sky. Declination figures are in degrees also.

Questions

1. Following the directions in the paragraphs above, what do you find is the average limiting magnitude in the different areas of your sky? According to these figures, how many constellations are completely lost at your site due to light pollution? How many are essentially lost (less than three stars visible)?

2. What are some of the most famous and interesting constellations lost from your site?

3. What are your results for constellations lost for other sites?

62.

Calculating Stars Lost

Find out the limiting magnitude for stars at your zenith or for stars at 45 degrees altitude in four different directions. Then, taking this figure or the average of the four figures, use Table 11 to estimate roughly how many stars you are losing to light pollution at your site (and other locations).

If we wish a very rough estimate of the number of stars we are losing to light pollution and (the unavoidable) atmospheric extinction at a site, we can do so easily. On a clear, moonless night, simply check out the limiting magnitude at your zenith. Then read from Table 11 to see how many total stars are brighter than that magnitude, and compare it to the total number in a naturally dark sky.

Of course, this crudest estimate fails to take into account atmospheric extinction—most stars at a given site do not pass near the zenith. And the gradient of dimming due to light pollution (or haze) is steeper down the sides of the sky than that due to atmospheric extinction alone. For greater accuracy, try finding the limiting magnitude of stars at 45 degrees altitude in four different directions, and then find the average of the four figures. Best of all, though, would be to map the isophotes across the entire night sky and figure out the number of square degrees of sky covered by each area of brightness. Besides being more precise, this would, I believe, usually show a still greater number of stars lost to light pollution.

Some people might argue that the stars we are losing are not much missed because they are the faintest ones anyway. But we do miss that overall spectacle of a star-sprinkled heaven. And brightness is not the only quality that can make a celestial object interesting or beautiful. (Consider some of the constellations—the subject of the previous activity.) Furthermore, if the argument goes that faint stars are not very interesting, then we should recall that light pollution is not only

Table 11
Number of stars brighter than various magnitudes

Magnitude	Number of Stars Brighter
−2.0	0
−1.0	1
0.0	4
1.0	16
2.0	45
3.0	150
4.0	540
5.0	1700
6.0	4900
6.5	8700
7.0	14,000

eradicating our view of faint stars, but also making the bright ones appear faint, to lose the beauty which gives them their identity as named wonders.

Questions

1. How many stars are lost to light pollution at your site according to the methods of using just the zenith limiting magnitude and of using the limiting magnitude at 45 degrees altitude in four different directions?

2. Can you determine limiting magnitudes all over the sky to make a map with isophotes and then figure out what percentage area of the sky is covered by each and how many stars are lost in each?

3. What are your results for number of stars lost at sites other than your own?

METEORS AND COMETS

63.

Studying the Full Duration of Major Meteor Showers

Observe the full duration of the major meteor showers. Make a graph of the rates over time. Find out what are the earliest and latest dates on which it is likely you are seeing a meteor belonging to that particular shower.

Meteors (also called shooting stars or falling stars) are the streaks of light we see when pieces of rock and iron from space called *meteoroids* burn up from their friction upon entering Earth's atmosphere at great speeds. When some of these meteors seem to come in greater quantity from a particular point (a *radiant*) in the heavens for a time, the event is called a *meteor shower,* a certain number of which occur every year on the same dates.

Many amateur astronomers have read about and observed some of the major meteor showers. But the observations are often limited to just the night that the shower is predicted to be at maximum. Yet, in most cases, the amount of time the Earth is passing through that particular *stream* of meteoroids in space is measured in days, sometimes weeks or even months. And much of the greatest scientific interest is in getting a full cross-section of the stream, whose density and type of meteoroidal particles (thus, also, type of meteor) may vary a lot along the course of that cross-section.

Thus the goal of this activity is to observe the full duration of the major meteor showers. Table 12 shows them with not only the supposed beginning and end dates indicated but also the beginning and end dates of the period during which they are supposed to be above *quarter-strength* (producing one-quarter or more the number of meteors they produce at maximum).

It seems to me that the incentive of trying to see the earliest Perseid or latest Geminid you can (or that anybody has) each year is a strong one, which has seldom, if ever, been suggested. Of course, there is one fairly clear reason it has not been suggested: Being 100 percent sure that any individual meteor you see is a member of a particular shower is essentially impossible for a single visual observer.

On the other hand, seeing several meteors appearing to come from the same radiant in one observing session would make the case stronger. It would be stronger still if the apparent speed, color, or other properties of the observed meteors were characteristic of the shower in question. These elusive and tricky furthest reaches of the showers are compelling. Remember, however, that the most scientifically valuable and satisfying achievement is to observe the entire duration of the shower well enough to make a good graph of the rates.

Here are a few final reminders for would-be meteor watchers. If you observe with other people, be sure to keep separate individual tallies of meteors. (If

Table 12
Major annual meteor showers

Shower	Maximum	Above One-Quarter Maximum*	Some Visible	Number per Hour §	Time**	Radiant §§
1. Quadrantids	Jan 4	Jan 4	Jan 1-6	40	6:00 A.M.	15h28m, +50°
2. Lyrids	Apr 22	Apr 21-23	Apr 18-25	15	12:00 A.M.	18h4m, +34°
3. Eta Aquarids	May 5	May 1-10	Apr 21-May 12	10	4:00 A.M.	22h30m, −2°
4. Delta Aquarids	Jul 29	Jul 19-Aug 8	Jul 15-Aug 29	25	2:00 A.M.	22h30m, 0° and 22h40m, −16°
5. Perseids	Aug 12	Aug 9-14	Jul 23-Aug 20	50	4:00 A.M.	3h4m, +58°
6. Orionids	Oct 21	Oct 20-25	Oct 2-Nov 7	25	4:00 A.M.	6h12.5m, +13.5° and 6h25m, +19.5°
7. Taurids	Nov 3	Oct 20-30	Sep 15-Dec 15	10	12:00 A.M.	3h32m, +14° and 4h16m, +22°
8. Leonids	Nov 18	Nov 16-20	Nov 14-20	5	5:00 A.M.	10h8m, +22°
9. Geminids	Dec 14	Dec 12-15	Dec 4-16	50	2:00 A.M.	7h28m, +32°
10. Ursids	Dec 22	Dec 21-23	Dec 17-24	10	5:00 A.M.	14h28m, +78°

* Period during which shower produces at least one-quarter of its maximum number of meteors per hour

§ Approximate number per hour for a well-placed observer with clear, dark skies at time of maximum

** Time (standard or daylight savings) when radiant is highest around date of maximum

§§ Radiant at date of maximum

127

someone's shout makes you wheel to spot a meteor you otherwise would not have seen, do not count it in your totals.) Keep track of the time carefully, noting totals for regular (not irregular) periods of time—half hour, one hour, and so on—if at all possible.

Questions

1. What are the earliest and latest dates on which you can make a good case that the meteors you see are members of a particular shower?

2. What does your graph of each shower's activity over its full duration show? How long before maximum does the shower reach quarter-strength and half-strength? How long after? Can you factor out the effects of moonlight and weather (both cloudy nights and nights with different amounts of haze) accurately enough to achieve a consistent curve on your graph? (Don't let your speculation overstep your data!)

64.

Studying Minor Meteor Showers

Observe the so-called minor meteor showers.

In *minor meteor showers*, fewer meteors per hour are seen than in the major showers—in fact, one or even none might be observed even in the best-chosen hour. Many amateur astronomers no doubt feel that is not enough return for the investment of time.

But this judgment overlooks several things. First of all, there are often several minor showers, part of a major shower, and good nonshower meteor activity going on during the same nights—plenty of entertainment! Second, an hour or two of watching for a minor meteor shower does not prevent you from browsing other kinds of celestial sights at the same time. Third, there is the greater relative importance of each meteor you see from a minor shower. You can almost make a minor meteor shower your own. Think of the thrill of witnessing a kind of meteor few people have knowingly seen before.

In short, the minor meteor showers are nearly unexplored phenomena about which anybody with patience and love of the heavens could make discoveries. Figure 13 and Table 13 provide information on what may be the most

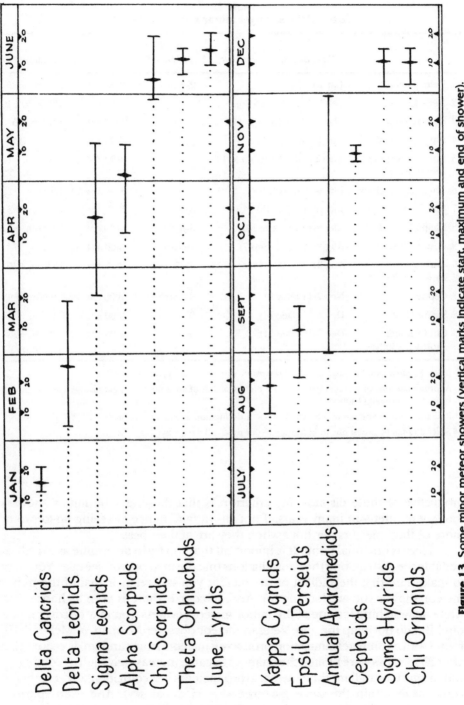

Figure 13 Some minor meteor showers (vertical marks indicate start, maximum and end of shower).

Table 13
Some of the stronger minor meteor showers

Name	Dates and Maximum Date	Number per Hour*	Time§	Radiant**
1. Delta Cancrids	Jan 13-21 (Jan 16)	2-3	12:00 A.M.	8h24m, +20
2. Delta Leonids	Feb 5-Mar 19 (Feb 26)	3	1:00 A.M.	10h36m, +19
3. Sigma Leonids	Mar 21-May 13 (Apr 17)	1 ++	11:00 P.M.	13h0m, −5
4. Alpha Scorpiids	Apr 11-May 12 (May 3)	8	3:00 A.M.	complex§§
5. Chi and (second) Alpha Scorpiids	May 27-Jun 20 (Jun 5 & 14)	5,5	1:00 A.M.	16h25m, −12 16h52m, −22
6. Theta Ophiuchids	Jun 8-16 (Jun 13)	2	1:00 A.M.	17h50m, −28
7. June Lyrids	Jun 10-21 (Jun 15)	8-10	2:00 A.M.	18h32m, +35
8. Kappa Cygnids	Aug 9-Oct 6 (Aug 18)	3-5	10:00 P.M.	19h20m, +55
9. Epsilon Perseids	Aug 21-Sep 16 (Sep 7)	10 (occ)	5:00 A.M.	4h8m, +37
10. Annual Andromedids	Aug 31-Nov 29 (Oct 3)	5-15 (occ)	2:00 A.M.	1h10m, +30
11. Cepheids	Nov 7-11 (Nov 9)	8 (rarely)	8:00 P.M.	23h30m, +63
12. Sigma Hydrids	Dec 3-15 (Dec 11)	9	3:00 A.M.	8h32m, +2
13. Chi Orionids (north & south)	Dec 4-15 (Dec 11)	6	1:00 A.M.	5h36m, +26 5h40m, +16

* Up to this rate around best hour of night at maximum, with clear and moonless country skies

§ Approximate time when radiant of shower is highest at date of maximum (daylight savings time if in month from April through October)

** Radiant in hours and minutes of RA, degrees of declination at date of maximum

§§ Several radiants, closest one to maximum at this time: 16h32m, −24

productive of these displays. My criterion is that these are the minor showers thought to offer—in many years, if not all—a fair chance of seeing up to two or more of their meteors per hour when they are at their best.

Here is one final point: It is important that you try to determine as exactly as possible the path among the constellations that the meteors you see take. You want to make sure that the radiant of the meteor you saw really is that of the minor meteor shower you are looking for. And, of course, there is even a chance that, while out watching for one of the minor meteor showers, you may discover a new one! But do not jump the gun. Veteran meteor observer Norman W. McLeod, III, found with a computer simulation producing meteors from random directions that after 25 meteors were plotted the chances became increasingly high of coming up with a spurious radiant for 2 meteors (two meteors just coincidentally seeming to come from within the same 2-degree-wide circle of sky). And even spurious radiants defined by 6 meteors (but not 7) of 40 observed were found, albeit rarely, in McLeod's 503 trials.

Questions

1. From how many of the minor showers can you see meteors this year? Which ones are more productive than our table lists? Which ones are less productive?

2. Do you find a different maximum date or radiant position than suggested? How many "sporadic" meteors do you see, and from where, while you look for one of the minor showers? Do you find evidence of a previously unknown shower in several meteors from an unlisted radiant?

65.

Watching for "Lost" and Nonannual Meteor Showers

On the dates when they are most likely to occur, watch for meteor showers that used to put on strong displays (or have only appeared on a few occasions but were then strong) and meteor showers that have been conjectured as existing but are not yet proven.

Without here exploring the technical reasons, we can say that there is always a chance of a formerly (or occasionally) glorious meteor shower returning to its former strength—at least for one more display. The point of this activity is to ensure that there will be observers watching when it does!

The notes below give information on some of the most interesting showers that have been strong at least once but are not strong (or even observed) every year. I have also added several conjectured showers that deserve to be looked for. For more details, refer to the latest year's *Astronomical Calendar* by Guy Ottewell. (See "Suggested Reading List.")

An asterisk below indicates that the shower is also a major annual one, for which radiant and other characteristics are given in Table 13 in the previous activity. For the other showers listed here, name, date, and radiant position are given first, then descriptive comments.

1. *March Geminids* (March 22–24) RA 6^{h}22^m, declination +23 degrees. Observed 1973 and 1975. *Zenithal Hourly rate* (rate you would see with 6.5 zenith limiting magnitude if radiant were at your zenith): up to 40.

2. *Lyrids** (April 21-22) Great displays in 1803, 1922 (96 per hour), and 1982 (more than 75 per hour).

3. *Grigg-Skjellerup meteors,* also called Pi Puppids (April 23) 7^h48^m −45 degrees. Very southerly for United States. Best chance every 5 years when Comet Grigg-Skjellerup returns; 1977 (38 per hour) and 1982 (23 per hour).

4. *Librids* (June 8-9) 15^h9^m −28 degrees. Seen only in 1937 (10 per hour).

5. *Sagittariids* (June 8-16) 20^h16^m −35 degrees. Only observed by radar and only in 1958 (30 per hour).

6. *Corvids* (June 25-30) 12^h48^m −19 degrees. Like Librids, seen only in 1937 and rate about 10 per hour.

7. *Pons-Winnecke meteors,* also called June Draconids, June Bootids, and Iota Dracondids (June 27-July 1) 15^h12^m +58 degrees or 15^h36^m +49 degrees. Comet Pons-Winnecke has 6.38-year orbit, last previous return 1989. One very strong display in 1916 (100 per hour).

8. *Upsilon Pegasids* (July 18-August 26; peak August 8) 23^h20^m +19 degrees. Rates 4 to 13 per hour—if it exists. Strongest in 1978?

9. *Talithids* (about August 20-26?) 8^h50^m +46 degrees. This shower is conjectured by the author on the basis of a 1982 fireball. (See pages 104–105 of *The Starry Room.*) Perhaps it consists of only great fireballs seen some years (including possibly 1783 and 1988).

10. *Aurigids* (August 31-September 1) 5^h38^m +42 degrees in 1935 (30 per hour); 6^h16^m +36.4 degrees in 1986 (many yellow meteors in a brief time).

11. *Draconids,* also called Giacobinids and October Draconids (October 7-10) 17^h28^m +54 degrees. Occasionally great, but brief displays when Comet Giacobini-Zinner (period 6.5 years) returns around October. Storms in 1933 and 1946. Strong display in 1985 for parts of the world.

12. *Cepheids* (November 7-11) 23^h30^m +63 degrees. Weak except in 1969.

13. *Andromedids,* also called Bielids (best chances for strong displays may be around November 14-15 and November 23-24). Radiant is 7- to-10-degree-wide area around 1^h40^m +44 degrees. Associated with Comet Biela, which was last seen, broken in two, in 1852. Meteor storms in 1872 and 1885; strong displays in 1892 and 1899. But little seen since then at this place and these dates. (The "annual Andromedids" are weak and peak earlier—early October.) Last notable activity in 1966.

14. *Leonids** (November 14-20). See Activity 66 for details.

15. *Monocerotids* (November 20-21). Radiant about 7^h15^m −7 degrees. Very intense in 1925 and 1935. Seen again in 1985.

16. *Phoenicids* (December 5) 1^h −45 degrees. Very southerly for United States. Only strong shower was in 1956 (100 per hour).

17. *Ursids** (December 17-24) 14^h28^m b1 . 78 degrees. Occasionally very strong, as in 1986 and especially in 1945 (110 per hour).

Questions

1. How many of the occasional (or "lost" or conjectured) meteor showers can you look for this year?

2. If you see any sign of what may be notable activity from one of the above showers, what are the numbers, times, exact radiants, and other properties of the meteors you observe?

66.

Monitoring the Leonids for Possible Meteor Storms

Watch carefully the full duration of the Leonid meteor shower each year, with especially great attention the closer we are to the next predicted Leonid storm years, 1998 and 1999.

The greatest meteor storms we know of in history have been those of Leonid meteors in or near the year of their parent comet's return. In 1799, 1833, 1866, and 1966 (and in several other years), the "stars fell like snowflakes," with rates in 1966 at Kitt Peak in Arizona rising up to as high as 140 meteors per second! Comet Tempel-Tuttle (period of 33.17 years) is due back in 1998, and a study by Donald K. Yeomans suggests that the Leonid displays in 1998 and 1999 have a good chance of being mighty ones. Furthermore, the Moon will not be in the sky for the key hours before dawn in either of those years.

Of course, on the other hand, the most intense part of the storm is brief enough to be visible from less than half the world at a given display. Will your part of the world be one of the lucky ones? At least we have two years, two chances, this time.

The most important point is that, even if the year in which you are reading these words is not 1998 or 1999, but some other year in the 1990s or 2000s, there is still plenty of reason to watch the Leonids.

The historic record shows that sometimes mighty Leonid displays have occurred many years before or after the comet's return—possibly even around the halfway point, when the comet is way out to the orbit of Uranus. Yeomans's work indicates that, even in our time, Leonid showers with rates of more than 100 meteors per hour seem to be possible for about a dozen years centered on the time of the comet's return.

133

So each year in the 1990s (and years afterwards), there is good reason to observe this usually quite modest shower.

Questions

1. How many Leonid meteors per hour do you observe on mid-November mornings this year? How does this compare with the totals of other observers and the rates observed (by yourself or others) last year?
2. Do you notice any unsual trends in the numbers of Leonids during your observing sessions? Do you notice any notable characteristics?

67.

Recording Meteor Brightness, Color, Trains, and Other Properties

Record not just numbers of meteors while observing a meteor shower (or meteors on a non-shower night), but also brightnesses, colors, trains, and other characteristics of the meteors.

The easiest task for meteor observers is just to count meteors. But, whether you use paper or audiotape to record your observations, here are some of the other interesting properties of meteors to find.

Brightness. Most people probably have a tendency to overestimate the brightness of meteors, which, unlike stars, are sudden, surprising, moving, and sometimes sizable. Make sure to account for atmospheric extinction by comparing a meteor with a star at a similar angular altitude. Ideally one should also note the altitude of the meteor—a meteor seen down near the horizon is many times farther away in the atmosphere than one seen overhead.

Speed. Time of the night is one major factor affecting meteor speed. The Taurids, from their radiant high in the evening sky, are quite "slow." The Leonids, from their radiant high at dawn, are "very swift." Early August meteor observers easily notice the difference between the "medium-slow" Delta Aquarids and the "swift" Perseids.

134

Meteor shower by a lighthouse.

Color. Meteors come in many colors, though of course the eye is not sensitive enough to distinguish color in the fainter ones. Speed is one determinant of the color (blue-white tending to be fast meteors and red tending to be slow meteors), but chemical composition plays a role, too. So there is more than just the aesthetic interest in recording colors.

Behavior. This term can cover the flares, splittings, explosions, and any pecularities of motion that the meteor undergoes in the course of its flight. An exploding meteor is called a *bolide*. Some meteors have a *terminal burst*. A few meteors at least appear to deviate from a straight course. Several meteors may follow parallel or otherwise similar flight paths, suggesting they are pieces of what was once (recently?) a single object.

Trains. Meteors may trail pieces and produce clouds of material. But the streak left behind after the meteor itself disappears is often a *train* caused by the ionization of atmospheric gases due to the meteor's high-velocity passage. Some showers have a much higher percentage of members with trains than do other showers. Although most trains endure very briefly, longer-lasting ones can occur and should be timed as well as possible. Rarely, a bright meteor's train may be visible long enough for its changing shape to be seen and sketched.

Time of Occurrence and Duration of Flight. Neither of these is crucial information unless the meteor is an extremely bright one; but they are interesting to note.

Other. Most scientifically valuable of all is to plot accurately the paths of meteors. But to do so requires much practice and also a star map with a *gnomonic projection*. These can be obtained from several places, but it is best to prove oneself as a diligent meteor watcher before undertaking the plotting challenge. (If you want to become such an observer, send a self-addressed, stamped envelope and a note expressing your interest to, David Meisel, Department of Physics and Astronomy, State University of New York at Geneseo, Geneseo, NY 14454.)

Question

1. How much information about the properties of an hour's worth of meteors can you record (on page or tape)?

2. What is the average magnitude of the meteors of a certain shower you observe during a session? Does there seem to be a most common color for them? What percentage of the meteors leave trains?

68.

Observing Fireballs and Gathering Fireball Observations

Be ready for fireball meteors, especially in early evening and in certain major meteor showers. When you see one, note and plot its path among the constellations or its angular altitude and azimuth along the path. Note all its characteristics. Encourage other local sky watchers to be alert and to report to you when they see a fireball. After a major fireball, solicit observations by letters to local newspapers. Send your results to SEAN and Meteor News.

A *fireball* is any meteor bright enough to outshine even Venus. I find that a person who observes the night sky even fairly often may see a meteor just bright enough to be a fireball each year. A fireball that outshines a half moon or even a full moon is rarer—but worth the wait!

What can you do to increase your chances of seeing fireballs? Most great fireballs are believed to be pieces from asteroids. All or most of the annual meteor showers are cometary, not asteroidal, in origin. If you are willing to settle for a few mere magnitude −5 (sometimes much brighter) meteors, though, there are a few showers that offer more fireballs. Our best all-around bet may be the Taurids of early November. (See Table 12.) Although it is yet unproven, I would also recommend the possible shower of presumably asteroidal fragments I call the Talithids. (See Activity 65.)

There is a complex interplay of factors that determines which one of 10,000,000 meteors will reach the ground and become a meteorite, but we can say that early evening is the best time for such meteors (which are all, of course, fireballs). In early evening, meteors are slower because Earth's rotation is then carrying the observer away from the direction of Earth's orbital motion. Early evening meteors are less likely to vaporize in a fraction of a second from being too fast.

What must you look for and remember in those few seconds that you do see a fireball? If you are able to notice exactly what the fireball's path was among the stars, your observation could be very valuable. On the other hand, partly cloudy skies, bright moonlight, twilight, or the brilliance of the fireball itself may render the background of stars unviewable. Then your hope is to recall the *azimuth* and *altitude* of the fireball in relation to objects in the landscape. (Be sure not to lose the exact location from which you saw the fireball or your line of sight to objects in the landscape will be all wrong!) For a good azimuth, you will need a compass. (This will actually give the magnetic azimuth—convertible to true azimuth for you later.) For a good angular altitude, you can try your fist at arm's length—though, actually, a special protractor or similar device is better.

In addition to determining the sky path, it is, of course, important to judge the brightness (were shadows cast plainly? If the Moon was up, how did the two compare?), apparent size of the head, color, any brightenings or bursts, but especially the position and manner in which the meteor ceased to be luminous (just vanished? terminal burst with no fragments? came apart into "sparks"?). Fireballs can leave incredibly long-lasting trains and debris clouds. Sketch and time them. And then, of course, there is that thrilling question: Did you hear any sound from the fireball? An ordinary sonic boom from a large fireball will usually reach you 1 or 2 minutes after the light from it did. (These objects are generally dozens of miles away at least.) If you hear the mysterious *anomalous sound*—sound simultaneous with the meteor's passage—fix in your mind what it was like and when it began and ceased.

Only observations from several locations can enable us to estimate the true path, brightness, and other properties of a fireball. If you know other sky watchers, arrange with them to report to you any fireball sightings they make or hear of. For a really spectacular fireball, you can try soliciting sightings through a letter to local newspapers. (Try the local science or nature columnist, if there is one.) Whatever you do, do swiftly. You will have enough trouble getting clear information from people about so stupefying an event; delay may make it hopeless.

When you have at least one good observation, send it to *Meteor News*. (See Suggested Reading List.) But the place you should send to most swiftly is SEAN— the Scientific Event Alert Network (National Museum of Natural History, Mail Stop 129, Washington, DC 20560). However, SEAN generally wants only fireballs at least as bright as a half-moon!

Questions

1. What is the path among the constellations, or the angular altitude and azimuth, of your fireball? What is its brightness, apparent size, color, train, manner of disappearance, and sound (if any)?

2. Can you obtain reports of fireballs from other local observers? By soliciting through letters to your local newspapers?

69.

Naked-Eye Observations and Brightness Estimates of Comets

Attempt to observe as many comets as possible with the naked eye. When you do observe one, make magnitude (and, if possible, apparent size) estimates. Compare these estimates with those derived by yourself or other people who used optical aid and various magnifications.

Most comets are faint and need to be pursued by telescope. But every few years, there is a comet distinctly visible to the naked eye. When there is, naked-eye observations of such an object are actually in several important ways superior to those with the telescope! Usually the head and sometimes the tail (see the next activity) of such a comet appear distinctly larger and brighter (of greater total brightness) viewed with the naked eye.

The quest to observe the size and brightness of a comet's head with the naked eye is therefore a significantly valuable one. But how is it possible that the naked eye can show us a brighter, larger comet if its light-gathering power is far less than that of binoculars and telescopes?

The answer lies in the nature of comets. The *coma* of a comet is a vast cloud of dust and gas, which is released from the relatively tiny (usually 1- to- 10-mile-wide) icy *nucleus* of the comet when the nucleus gets close enough in toward the Sun in space for its surface to start vaporizing. (Actually this surface *sublimates*—passes directly from solid to vapor—due to the vacuum of space.) It is nucleus (too small and/or shrouded to be seen) and coma that together make up the *head* of a comet. And what is the reason the naked eye can see more of the coma (and thus a greater total brightness of it) than telescopes? The outer regions of the coma are already so thinly spread that the magnification of telescopes (even of binoculars) spreads them out beyond the limits of perception—the surface brightness becomes too low to see.

How much larger a diameter will the coma have and how much brighter will it be with the naked eye compared to optical instruments? The answers will vary greatly depending on the particular optical instruments and sky conditions. Walter Scott Houston has mentioned how he saw with the naked eye the coma of the close-passing Comet IRAS-Araki-Alcock vary from an amazing 2 degrees across to a stupendous (in fact, record) 6 degrees across over periods of 10 to 30 minutes—due to changing atmospheric conditions. Furthermore, the difference in size and brightness between the naked-eye views and the telescopic views will also depend on the comet. Presumably, by making naked-eye observations of a comet on a number of nights and comparing these with telescopic observations (by yourself or other people) from the same locale on the same nights, you can isolate the role played by the coma's structure itself—learning some important information about the comet. (Of course, the coma of a comet can itself vary over time, but usually not too drastically over a short period of time.)

Remember that, when you read of a comet being predicted to reach, say, magnitude 7—normally too faint for an extended (nonpoint source) object to be glimpsed with the naked eye—this figure is really the prediction for a certain standard size of telescope (a telescope of 2.7-inches aperture, because this was the average size of telescopes in Bobrovnikoff's study in the 1940s of this so-called *aperture effect*). A comet that is magnitude 7 to a small telescope might be more like magnitude 6 or even magnitude 5 to the naked eye. Of course, if the comet (that is to say, its head) is large, it is not strictly comparable to the nearly point sources that are stars—not without some special technique to make more similar their apparent size. Wearers of eyeglasses can experiment with glasses off to see if this makes star and comet out-of-focus images closer in size. It is also possible to try comparing comets with deep-sky objects of similar apparent size.

Do not forget to seek the darkest, clearest skies possible and to use averted vision when looking for a faint comet. Will you be able to estimate its size with the naked eye? There might seem to be few good comparison objects of known size. But one possibility is to compare it to the apparent width of the ray-spread of a first-magnitude star. The latter is probably no more than about 2 arc-minutes wide to most viewers under usual conditions. If your comet is vastly larger than that, you might use one of the largest, brightest deep-sky objects for comparison—though the naked-eye size of most of these is not well known.

Questions

1. At what predicted magnitude (for a 2.7-inch telescope) does a particular comet first become visible to the naked eye for you? How much difference is there, for each comet, between this predicted standard telescope magnitude and the naked-eye magnitude you determine?

2. How much larger do the heads of different comets look to the naked eye than they do with various binoculars and telescopes?

70.

Naked-Eye Observations of Comet Tails

When a bright comet's tail is visible to the naked eye, observe it without optical aid and estimate the length (and width) of it. Note how your figures compare with those derived from binocular and telescopic observations on the same nights under similar conditions.

The previous activity explained why the naked eye is sometimes able to see a greater extent and total brightness of a comet's head than binoculars or telescope can. That information applies every bit as much—or more—for the tenuous but enthralling part of a comet known as the tail.

Tails, the trademarks of comets, are actually not found on some of them. And although any comet head bright enough to be seen with the naked eye will almost certainly have a tail, the tail itself may not be bright enough to see without optical aid. For instance, some very bright comets with magnificent tails have had the tails fade from naked-eye view when the comet (its head) was still as bright as third magnitude. On the other hand, a few comets have had great lengths of tails with as high a surface brightness as the brighter part of the coma. Each comet will present a different case for you to study.

Even rarer than getting a comet with a good naked-eye tail is getting one in which several tails or several parts of the tail are visible. The straight, narrow tail, which points almost exactly away from the Sun, is the *gas* (or *plasma*) *tail*. The curved, broad tail, which lags behind this antisunward line, is the *dust tail*. We may often see the dust tail from an angle such that its curve is not evident. Quite often, the dust and gas tails are superimposed one on the other as seen from our point of view. Occasionally, though—as in the case of 1976's superb Comet West—the two tails appear well separated and bright enough to study well with the naked eye. Comet West was one of those rare examples of a comet whose tails even showed a little color (gas tail, blue; dust tail, yellow) to the unaided eye.

But make no mistake about: With certain bright comet's tails, the naked eye can sometimes outperform optical aid or even the best photographs in perceiving the longest extent of tail. (This may have been the case, or nearly the case, with Comet Halley in 1986 and IRAS-Araki-Alcock in 1983.) So find a dark site and a clear night, and use your averted vision. Do not be biased by any expectations. Look carefully and repeatedly. You may perceive merely the edge of tail where the gradient of its brightness falls off to that of the dark sky. Perhaps your naked eye will reveal more of this ghostly visitor than anything else or anyone else in the world does!

Questions

1. How bright must the comet itself be before you can see its tail? How many degrees long can you trace the tail? How does this compare with what is seen with optical aid?

2. What kinds of tail does this particular comet have? Is the comet's orientation such that you can see both gas tail and dust tail? (The gas tail's light is mostly emitted near the violet end of human perception—compare the gas tail length estimates of different people in the same observing conditions to see how much they differ. Is age a factor?)

RAINBOWS, HALOS, CORONAS, AND GLORIES

71.

Studying and Timing a Rainbow's Changes

Study the visibility of different parts of a rainbow (including the secondary bow, if seen) during a display. Time changes in the visibility and in the relative prominence of colors. Have several people drive to different sites, and carry out these studies at the same time to see what differences the change in place makes.

When sunlight shines on raindrops in the part of the sky opposite from the Sun, the light reflected back to the observer also gets refracted (bent) during its passages between the two mediums (air and water). The different wavelengths of the light (the different colors) are refracted by different amounts, so we see all the colors displayed in a band. Why is that band 40½ to 42 degrees from the anti-solar point (the point exactly opposite the Sun, as far below the horizon as the Sun is above)? Because that angle is the *angle of minimum deviation* (product of the laws of reflection and refraction)—no light from (a single) reflection escapes the drops higher in the sky than here, so this is the edge at which the colors do not wholly overlap and can be seen separately.

You might see many rainbows this summer if you remember the rules of the rainbow—for instance, that the Sun must be lower than 42 degrees for the primary rainbow to be in the sky. But even if you only see a single occurrence of the rainbow this year, that rainbow may be like many in one. While visible, its appearance may change radically many times. The changes are so smooth that the observer—already awestruck—may have trouble keeping track of them.

You can keep track better if you have some specific features you know to look for in advance. The next activity concentrates on the colors of the bow and Activity 73, on such things as supernumerary arcs and Alexander's dark band. When you have read these activities and get a chance to do them, you will be able to bring them all together for the current activity: a full description of a rainbow and its changes.

Take notes and photographs (though the photos may show the bow somewhat differently than you saw it), and do so at each stage in a rainbow display. The effort to keep up with the bow's changes will make you see and appreciate more.

And suppose you have a second bow to follow at the same time? The secondary bow is about 11 degrees farther out from the anti-solar point than the primary bow is. Note that the secondary bow is roughly twice as wide as the primary bow and has the order of its colors reversed.

By the way, another possibility for studying the rainbow is to drive a few miles (or a fraction of a mile) during the course of its occurrence to examine how the change in your position in space affects the bow's appearance. In order to distinguish these changes from those occurring anyway at a fixed site, you should leave companions at the original site (or several sites), and everyone involved should keep track of the exact time changes occur.

Questions

1. How long a time is at least part of the rainbow visible? Which portions of it are strongest at different times in the display? Which colors are strongest, which weakest or absent, at different times in the display? If visible, at what times and places in the sky are effects like supernumerary arcs (see Activity 73) most and least prominent?

2. If the secondary bow is visible, can you answer about it the same questions as asked in question 1? To what extent (if any) can you correlate its features and changes to those of the primary bow?

3. Most important of all, can you judge to what extent each rainbow's features and changes are a result of size of the raindrops (see the next activity), amount of Sun and rain, distance to the rain from the observer, and clearness of air?

72.

Studying a Rainbow's Colors

See how many distinct colors you can distinguish in a rainbow at any given time, finding which is strongest and which is widest. If you do not detect all seven of the famous colors, note which are missing. Compare your results to the independent color judgment of other people observing right beside you. If the rain causing the bow is still falling around you or has just passed, record anything you can about amount of rain (for example, heaviness of the shower) and the size of the raindrops; use that information with Table 14 to see if it helps explain the colors observed.

We hear of the famous seven colors of the rainbow, but usually we cannot distinguish that many distinct hues. On the other hand, might it sometimes be possible to distinguish more than seven? The colors blend into each other, and it might be possible to distinguish several shades of red or other major color.

The first set of actors determining what colors are reported in a rainbow

Table 14
Rainbow characteristics produced by different raindrop sizes
(after M. Minnaert)

Raindrop Diameter (Millimeters)	Description
1.0–2.0	Rainbow with very bright violet and vivid green, pure red, scarcely any blue. Pink and green supernumerary arcs are numerous (as many as five) and merge into the primary bow but begin to overlap and become difficult to distinguish if raindrops are much more than 1-millimeter wide.
0.5	Red weaker in primary bow. Fewer supernumeraries, but they are still pink and green.
0.2–0.3	No more red, but rest of bow broad and well developed. Supernumeraries pale and yellowish.
< 0.2	A gap between primary bow and first supernumerary arc.
0.08–0.1	Bow broad and pale, only violet vivid. First supernumerary well separated from primary and is whitish.
0.06	Primary bow contains a distinct white stripe.

come from the observer. Observers vary as to how well they can notice and name different hues, and the reasons are both biological and cultural. That is to say, there are differences in both people's physiological ability to perceive colors and their verbal ability to describe those colors in language. Consequently, it would be very interesting to have several people observing a rainbow right beside you and forming their own judgments of the colors independently. Most people forget one of the seven colors—indigo—and do not know that it is supposed to lie between violet and blue. Would such people tend not to notice three discrete hues in this part of the rainbow (blue, indigo, and violet) even while a person who knew indigo did?

The second set of factors is in the outside world. The prominence with which any of the colors is seen naturally varies with the amount of sunlight and rain and the clearness of the air. But very important is the size of the raindrops. The size makes a difference in the colors of the bow, and in the appearance of supernumerary arcs. (In the next activity, see the discussion of why size of the droplets matters and why the rainbow's colors can never be quite pure.) Table 14 (adapted from Minnaert) gives the colors and supernumerary arcs to be expected from raindrops of various sizes. Try to see if you can verify these predictions with your own observations. The easiest would be a rainbow produced by rain very near to you that was still spattering (or had just spattered) you with noticeably large drops.

As one final point about this violet, bottom part of the primary bow, note that it is often bordered, still farther down in the sky, by supernumerary arcs, whose colors should not be confused with the main ones of the bow. These arcs are a topic of our next activity.

Questions

1. What is the number and identity of the hues that you see in a rainbow at a given point and time? Which hue is widest? Which is strongest? Which are absent?

2. How do your answers to question 1 compare to those of a person observing with you? If they are different, can you trace them to a difference in the two observers' eyesight or in their color vocabulary?

3. If you can determine the probable raindrop size causing a particular bow, do you find that the bow's colors are indeed as predicted for that size? If not, why not?

73.

Supernumerary Arcs and Alexander's Dark Band

During each rainbow display, note whether Alexander's dark band is prominent, and determine why or why not. More importantly, look for supernumerary arcs, and study their number, color, and spacing.

The light causing the primary rainbow has been reflected only once inside raindrops. Activity 71 stated that none of this light, after being refracted and reflected, and refracted again ends up coming out at an angle greater (higher in the sky) than the primary rainbow. Plenty of this once-reflected light, however, comes out lower in the sky. Even though with all the colors overlapping it appears as just whitish light, this whitish light makes the sky below the primary bow often appear strikingly brighter than the dark sky above the bow.

The dark-sky region above the primary rainbow is sometimes called *Alexander's dark band* (after Alexander of Aphrodisias, who described it long ago). It is a band because it is bounded on top by the secondary rainbow (whether or not this becomes bright enough to be visible) and by bright sky above the secondary rainbow. Why is the sky especially bright above the secondary? Because just as the primary bow is the upper edge of all light emerging back out of raindrops after one internal reflection, so the secondary bow is the lower edge (in the sky) of all light emerging back out of the raindrops after two internal reflections.

The stronger the sunlight and rain, the more intense the rainbow and the more likely you will see a prominent display of Alexander's dark band. But it is not quite that simple. For one thing, the sky around the rainbown may also appear dark and light—but in different places than the band phenomenon produces—due to the distribution of clouds. At each rainbow, try to explain the extent to which Alexander's dark band is or is not visible.

More variable and interesting than the dark band are *supernumerary arcs*. These appear as extra bands of color just below the violet at the bottom of the primary rainbow (and, very rarely, just above the violet at the top of the secondary). They require a more sophisticated description of light than merely considering it to consist of rays. They prove that light has a waveform. Figure 14 shows one ray (drawn darker than the others) emerging from a raindrop at the rainbow angle, other rays at less extreme angles. We can see that, although all emerge in the same general direction (towards an imaginary observer), the distance each travels within

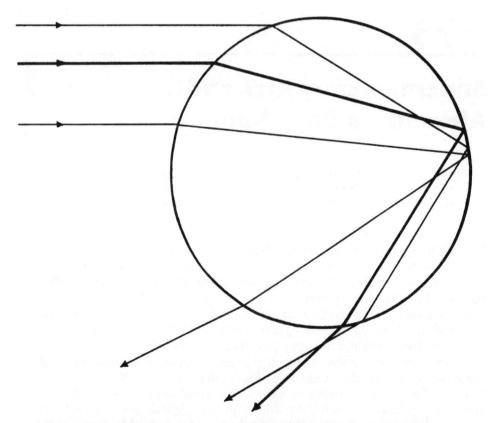

Figure 14 Path of light rays through a raindrop (thicker line is ray that leaves at angle of minimum deviation).

the raindrop is different. Now if these rays are really waves, all entering the drop *in phase* (their crests and troughs lined up side by side) but the waves have different distances to travel within the raindrops, some of them are going to exit out of phase with each other. A wave that traverses a distance in the drop ½ a wavelength less than, or 1½ or 2½ wavelengths more than, the distance of another wave, will exit perfectly out of phase with it; the two will leave crest to trough, and therefore canceling each other out, an example of *destructive interference.* On the other hand, those waves traveling 1, 2, 3, and so on wavelengths more distance than another wave will reinforce the light intensity—*constructive interference.* And thus, just under the primary rainbow, we will sometimes see strips of light and dark—or we would if it were not for one more twist.

Different colors are of different wavelengths. And so the strips in which the longer, red-end wavelengths would be absent due to destructive interference are the very ones that may be filled with shorter, violet-end wavelengths due to constructive interference—and vice versa. Usually, if color is visible, we see supernumerary arcs as alternating strips of pale pink and pale blue or green.

Now it is easy to understand why, in Table 14 in the previous activity, there is a different appearance of supernumerary arcs (and slightly different colors in the primary) for each drop size. But there are a few additional factors that determine the visibility of and precise colors of the supernumerary arcs. The drops in a shower are not all of exactly the same size. The farther a shower departs from the ideal of uniform drop size, the more the different wavelengths will overlap haphazardly and the less the arcs will be colorful or even distinguishable.

Questions

1. Can you see Alexander's dark band during a rainbow display? If not, or if it is not prominent, what distribution of bright and dark from clouds is responsible for concealing or confusing the effect?

2. How many supernumerary arcs can you see below the primary bow? What are their color and their spacing from the primary bow (if any)? If supernumeraries are not visible with a bright bow, what is the reason?

74.

Looking for Moon Rainbows and Higher-Order Rainbows

Look for rainbows caused by the Moon. During a daytime rainbow display, look for the rainbows of higher order.

Besides the famous primary and secondary rainbows and the supernumerary arcs, there are many other kinds of rainbows or rainbow-related phenomena. The not-so-rare phenomena called fogbows and dewbows and the marvelous, mind-boggling sun-reflection bows we will deal with in activities of their own. But the present activity consists of specifically looking for the other, much less frequent rainbow phenomena, at the times and places they are most likely to appear. Admittedly, most of our attempts to see them will be failures. But knowing when and where to look, as so very few people do, will greatly increase our chances.

First of all is the *moon rainbow*—a rainbow caused by moonlight rather than sunlight. The problem here is the Moon's relative dimness. Moon rainbows will only be possible when the Moon is fairly near full. Even then they will rarely show much color, simply because the brightness of the bow will not be strong enough to activate the color-sensing cells in our retinas. Notice I say that such bows will rarely show much color. In parts of the Hawaiian Islands, conditions for rainbows are so excellent that moon rainbows may show color far more often—as was claimed by Mark Twain and as I recently had verified by a present-day resident of Hawaii I know (He claims to see a rainbow about every other day!)

The other unusual kinds of rainbow to look for in this activity are the rainbows of *higher order*. These are the 3rd, 4th, 5th, and so on rainbows—the bows caused not by 1 reflection in raindrops like the primary, or by 2 reflections, like the secondary, but by three, four, five, or even more reflections.

The rareness of these bows may at first seem utterly discouraging. Many of these bows have been seen in indoor experiments, but in nature itself, the sightings are a mere handful—with only a few of that handful sounding very convincing. Just a few years ago, an excellent sighting of the third rainbow was reported (see the December 1986 issue of *Weather*), and perhaps other people have seen it. But of the other bows, I know of only the claimed sightings of the 5th bow by the nineteenth century rainbow researcher Eleuthere Mascart.

These higher-order rainbows may be far more common than we think, however. After all, the number of people who even know of their existence, let alone where to look for their dim traces, must be exceedingly small. I hope that this book will help change that. Whenever a rainbow display begins, have in mind at least the positions of the 3rd, 4th, and 5th bows. The 5th-order rainbow, though fainter than the 3rd and 4th, is at least projected against the otherwise dark

Table 15
**Rainbows of orders 1 through 8 and their angular
distance from the anti-solar point (in degrees*)**

Rainbow	Red	Violet	Order of Colors
1	42	40	red/violet
2	51	54	violet/red
3	139	143	violet/red
4	136	130	red/violet
5	52	45	red/violet
6	32	41	violet/red
7	116	126	violet/red
8	158	170	violet/red

* Based on calculations by Kotelnikov. (See page 270 in Boyer's *The Rainbow, From Myth to Mathematics.*)

background of Alexander's dark band. (See the previous activity.) Note that the 3rd and 4th bows are back in the general direction of the Sun, where the sky is brighter and where you must know your halo phenomena (see Activities 78 through 85) if you are not to be fooled into mistaking one for a higher-order rainbow. Table 15 lists the computed approximate positions and sizes of the first 10 bows. Exactly where they appear in nature may be a little different, but not enough to defeat our purposes.

Is there a lesser-known rainbow than any of these? There is the marvelous rainbow of zero order—but that is a topic I will save for an upcoming book!

Questions

1. Are you missing opportunities to look for moon rainbows? If you see one, does it show any color? What are the circumstances?

2. Can you glimpse a trace of any of the rainbows of higher order? What are the details of your sighting if you think you have succeeded?

75.

Sun-Reflection Rainbows and the Rainbow's Reflection

When a rainbow appears, get to a body of calm water to study and photograph the reflection of the rainbow. Look also for sun-reflection rainbows caused by the reflected image of the Sun in water shining on rain.

Our first effect can be seen virtually any time that the primary rainbow is visible— as long as you have a still body of water nearby to look into. I refer to the reflection of the rainbow. The colossally strange thing about this reflection is that it is not of the rainbow you are simultaneously seeing above it in the sky! The reflection you see on the water is actually of the rainbow that an observer out on that spot in the water would see. If the spot is fairly far away from you, the raindrops causing the bow visible from there could be very different from the one you (on the shore) are seeing in the sky. Therefore, it is always a good idea to check the reflection of the rainbow carefully. Are the colors and their relative prominence the same? Are the same sections visible? Even if the reflection appears essentially the same as the rainbow in the sky, of course, its different background will set it off somewhat differently: the colors of all things are richer and warmer when seen reflected in water.

Quite rare in most locales—but not necessarily in all—is what we may distinguish from the reflection of the rainbow by calling the *sun-reflection rainbow*. This is a rainbow in the sky caused by the bright reflected image of the Sun on water. Many of the strangest rainbow displays can be explained by this mechanism. The sun-reflection bow will always be higher in the sky than the primary bow, save when the Sun is on the horizon and the two coincide. The formula for height of the top of the sun-reflection bow is simply $x + 42$ degrees, in which x is the altitude of the Sun. Another way to figure it is to realize that the difference between the height of the primary bow's top and that of the sun-reflection bow is twice that of the Sun's altitude. Thus if the Sun is 10 degrees high, the top of the sun-reflection bow is $10 + 42$, or 52, degrees high, which is $2 \times 10 = 20$ degrees higher than the top of the primary bow (32 degrees high). From these calculations, it can be seen that when the primary bow is on the horizon, the top of the sun-reflection bow is 84 degrees high, and the full circle of it, 42 degrees in radius, could be visible! But even that is not the final extreme. Even if the Sun were too high to cause the primary bow (for a ground-based observer), a sun-reflection bow might be seen! Considering all this information, observers should scan the sky in the position that a dim sun-reflection bow might be visible—maybe even when it is raining with the Sun out but over 42 degrees above the horizon.

I have another, daring thought about sun-reflection bows: Under excellent circumstances, might not a person create one with a mirror?

Questions

1. During a rainbow display, can you see a rainbow reflection in a body of calm water? Besides the colors looking darker and warmer, do you notice any differences between them and those of the rainbow then above them in the sky? If so, what are the differences? Are all the same sections visible in the sky also visible in the reflection?

2. If you notice an odd rainbow, can it be explained as a sun-reflection bow? When an "ordinary" rainbow occurs—or even if it does not but there is Sun and rain—can you see any trace of a sun-reflection bow in the expected position? What colors in what widths do you see?

76.

Fogbows

Look for fogbows, and record how wide each is, how much of it is visible, and what color, if any, is visible in it. Most importantly, measure the angular distance of the fogbow from the anti–light-source point (marked by the shadow of the observer's head). Also be sure to check for the presence of supernumerary arcs and a secondary fogbow.

On a foggy night, with a streetlight at your back on a country road, you will often have the eerie experience of seeing a white arch of light ahead of you. It recedes as you approach it and finally fades from view when you get too far from the streetlight. The same experience can be had sometimes with the rising Sun at your back on a foggy morning. In both cases, the ghostly arch is a *fogbow*—the rainbow phenomenon occurring in fog.

The most obvious difference between rainbows and fogbows is the latter's lack of color. Sometimes a trace of orange may be seen on the top of the fogbow, blue, on the bottom. But usually the entire bow appears white. The explanation lies in the minuteness of fog droplets. The size of these droplets is closer than raindrops to the size of light's wavelengths. When light waves encounter an aperture or particle that is close enough to their own size, *diffraction* causes them to spread out and, thus, the various colors to overlap each other. The result is white light, spread out to as much as twice the angular width of the rainbow's band.

A wonderful aspect of fogbows is their ability to sometimes be visible as complete circles. Only from an airplane or high elevation is there likely to be enough rain between an observer and the ground to produce a full-circle rainbow. (In fact, I am unaware of there being any photo of such a rainbow in nature.) But there can fairly often be enough fog between a standing (even a sitting or lying) person and the ground for a fogbow to form. When you see the prominent arch, look carefully to discover if you can make out the bottom part that completes the circle. Try to find the best distance from the streetlight (if that is your light source) and the darkest background (quite important for seeing fogbows). You will probably notice the visibility of the bow changing with changes in the passing fog, too, so keep watching.

In addition to noting how much of the fogbow is visible and the width of the band and whether there is any color in it, you should determine the distance of the band from the anti-solar point (or, if the bow is caused by a streetlight or car headlights, the *anti-light-source point!*). That point is located at the shadow of the observer's head. In fogbows, the distance from the point to the bow is less than 42 degrees, less than in rainbows. And it is variably less—the smaller the fog droplets, the smaller the radius of the fogbow circle or arch.

Finally, you should look for and measure distance from anti-solar points of supernumerary arcs and secondary fogbows. The latter are supposedly rare, but I have seen one. There are several interesting features of the fogbow's super-numerary arcs. For one thing, they can be located quite a distance closer to the anti-solar point than to the primary fogbow. They tend to be more prominent compared to the primary than is the case with rainbows. And in fogbows, the first supernumerary is pinkish or reddish and the second, greenish or bluish—the opposite from the situation in rainbows. Be sure to note everything you can about these phenomena when you see them.

Questions

1. Can you see a bow in tonight's or this morning's fog with a streetlight or the Sun at your back? How much of the full circle can you see? Is there any orange on top or blue on bottom of the arch's band? How wide is the band? How many degrees is it from the anti-light-source point?

2. Does your fogbow display any supernumeraries? If so, how many and what is their color and distance from the primary fogbow? Do you see a secondary fogbow? What is its angular distance and other attributes?

77.

Dewbows

Look for dewbows, noting their apparent shape and colors. Also look for secondary dewbows and sun-reflection dewbows.

Dewdrops on a lawn or grassy field may reflect and refract the light of the Sun and cause a *dewbow.* As with the rainbow and the fogbow, the observer must have his or her back to the light source. In one way, the dewbow is more like the rainbow than the fogbow is: Almost always, the size of the dewdrops is large enough to form a colorful bow. But the startling thing is that the dewbow typically is seen not in the form of a circle or part of a circle, but as a hyperbola (wide-open curve) whose arms widen as they recede away from us!

This strange shape is of course only a result of the locating of the drops in a horizontal plane. Only if the dew remains until the Sun is high may we see the wide-open curve of the hyperbola close to form an ellipse. That is a rare sight to hope for. But there is probably a better chance of detecting a secondary dewbow, if you know in what position it might be glimpsed: in a hyperbola like the primary's but located a little closer to the observer.

On the other hand, a dewbow caused by the reflected image of the Sun—what we might call a *sun-reflection dewbow*—is located farther from the observer, forming a smaller hyperbola than the primary dewbow. But how could a reflected image of the Sun shine up on dew the way it can on rain? The answer is, by shining up from a pond upon whose surface—no, just above whose surface—dewdrops float!

I have read a rather unclear reference to just one instance of supernumerary arcs having been observed with a dewbow. I cannot think of a likely reason why they should be very rare. They should lie farther from the observer than the primary and so might be confused with the sun-reflection bow when observed on water.

Even more strangely shaped dewbows may be seen by an observer standing looking down on dew with a streetlight high over his or her head.

Wherever you spot dewbows, it is a worthy and—due to how little known they are—original activity just to observe them and record all facts about their appearance.

Questions

1. Can you see a dewbow on a suitable grassy, sunlit surface not long after sunrise this morning? How long after sunrise can you observe it? What colors does it display?

2. Can you spot a secondary dewbow or supernumerary arcs with a dewbow? On a pond at dawn, can you see a sun-reflection dewbow? At night on dewy grass under a streetlight, can you see a strangely shaped dewbow?

78.

Twenty-Two-Degree Halos

Keep a record of how often you see at least part of the 22-degree halo around the Sun or Moon. Keep track of how often a major rainfall occurs within 12 to 24 hours after you see a full or conspicuous 22-degree halo. Note how much of the full circle is visible, whether any color is apparent, what the altitude of the Sun is, and whether any other halo phenomena are present.

Halo phenomena are numerous kinds of rings, arcs, columns, and patches of light in the sky produced when sunlight or moonlight is refracted and/or reflected at certain angles by ice crystals. These ice crystals are usually miles above ground level in clouds of the cirrus types. The reason why concentrations of light appear in certain places is the same as with the rainbow—only here it is the refraction and reflection (in some halo effects, only reflection) by ice crystals, which results in rays entering a particular side of a crystal and exiting at never less than a minimum angle of deviation (at which angle many rays and, thus, an intensification of light occurs). If refraction is involved, a few colors or even all the rainbow colors may be visible.

By far the most popularly known halo phenomena is the *ring around the Moon* (or Sun), technically known as the *22-degree halo*—due to the angular radius of the huge circle it forms. Sometimes it is also called the *small halo* (due to there being an even huger halo, as discussed in Activity 84). "Ring around the Moon means rain soon," is an old weather saying, and it should fairly often be proven true due to the fact that the full ring will often be seen in the abundant cirrus or cirrostratus clouds that typically precede a warm front or other system that brings with it rain over vast areas. Test how often substantial rain occurs within 12 or 24 hours after you see a lunar 22-degree halo or a solar 22-degree halo.

Once you know the kinds of clouds that cause these halos and the fact that they do occur with the Sun, you will probably find yourself seeing far more solar halos than lunar. Most people avoid looking even in the general direction of the Sun, even though 22 degrees from it (especially when clouds may dim it) is quite safe. You will be amazed at how often you see at least a section of the small halo. (Do not confuse it with a cloud corona, best known as truly small—several degree wide—bands of color directly adjacent to the Moon. See Activity 85.) But it is a

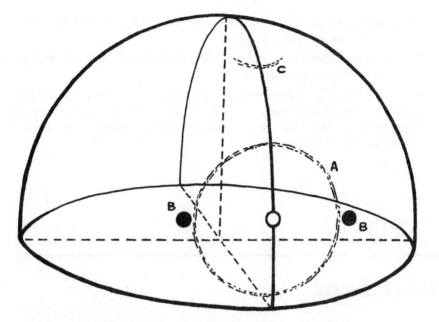

Common halo phenomena: A—22-degree halo; B—mock suns; C—circumzenithal arc.

seldom-performed experiment to keep track of how many halos you actually do see in a week, month, and year. This is truly valuable scientific information, so try the task. You should see at least dozens a year (of at least partial displays) in most climates.

The colors of the 22-degree halo are seldom very prominent when caused by the relatively weak light of the Moon. But in solar halos, you will often see red on the inner edge, blue on the outer edge. Seldom are many more colors visible, unless it seems to be in a section at the top of the halo, but may be really due to what is called the upper tangential arc, part of the circumscribed halo. (See Activity 82.) Note the colors and also that the inner edge of the halo is sharp, the outer edge, diffuse, and the sky encircled by the halo darker than that outside it—all features that are explained in the same way as Alexander's dark band in the rainbow. (See Activity 73.)

You should note any other halo phenomena you see with the small halo, of course. And the dependence of some of these other phenomena's appearance— even their absence or presence—on the Sun's altitude is one of the reasons you should always note how high up the Sun is when you observe the 22-degree halo.

Questions

1. How many times a year can you see part of a 22-degree halo around the Sun? Around the Moon? (What is the smallest lunar phase at which you see a halo?)

How often do you see the entire 22-degree solar or lunar halo? Is any particular time of year best for them, or worst?

2. How often is a prominent display of the solar or lunar halo followed within 12 or 24 hours by a substantial rainfall?

3. What sections of a 22-degree halo are visible in a particular display? What colors? Do you notice whether the sky encircled by the halo is darker? (If not, why not?) What other halo phenomena (if any) are visible at the time? What is the altitude of the Sun then?

79.

Mock Suns

Keep record of how often you see mock suns. Note the Sun's altitude and how far the mock sun is located from the Sun or from the 22-degree halo (if the latter is present). Note the colors and brightness of each mock sun and whether it possesses a "tail." Write down what other halo phenomena (if any) are visible while the mock sun is.

A *mock sun,* or *sun dog,* or (most technically) *parhelion* (plural, *parhelia*) is a patch of ice-crystal-caused light found at the same altitude as the Sun but at least 22 degrees right or left of the Sun—in other words, at least as far from the Sun as the 22-degree halo. It is actually when the Sun is on the horizon that mock suns are located right on the 22-degree halo. At higher solar elevations, the mock suns get farther and farther away from the Sun until disappearing at solar elevations higher than 61 degrees. Seldom are mock suns seen with the Sun nearly so high, so observations are needed.

The mock sun's brightness and color may be far greater than that of the 22-degree halo, and mock suns may be just about as common. Or are they? You can find out. Whenever a mock sun is dazzling, you should check to see if it causes shadows! Its colors are at least red (on the side towards the Sun) and blue (on the side away from the Sun)—sometimes extremely vivid and sometimes with all the other spectral colors between them.

Be sure to note these colors, the Sun's altitude, and the mock sun's distance from the Sun or 22-degree halo. (The latter may or may not be present; just one or both mock suns may be seen.) But also look for a *tail* on every mock sun, or sun dog, you see. This bluish-white tail is a streak emerging from the blue side of the mock sun and pointing away from the Sun at the same altitude. Can it be longer the higher the solar elevation? These tails can be quite, long but it is easy to confuse them with the parhelic circle. (See Activity 84.)

How is it that such strange patches of light can be produced by ice crystals? The 22-degree halo occurs in long "pencil" or squat "plate" forms of hexagonal ice crystals floating at random orientations. But the mock suns occur only with the plate crystals and only when these are floating with their bases nearly horizontal. Diagrams of the paths of light through the crystals for these and other halo phenomena can be found in halo expert Robert Greenler's book *Rainbows, Halos, and Glories.*

Questions

1. How often can you see mock suns? What is the solar elevation and what is their distance from the Sun when you see them? How bright are they? What colors are visible?

2. Do you observe any tail on the mock sun? How long is it, and what is the solar elevation? What other halo phenomena (if any) are visible when you see a particular mock sun display?

80.

Sun Pillars and "Double Suns"

Watch for sun pillars, and find out how often you can see one extending up (sometimes down) from a low (or even below-the-horizon) Sun. Note the Sun's altitude or time when you first notice a pillar, when it is most visible, and when you last see it. Measure the length of the pillar(s). Note what other halo phenomena (if any) are visible at the same time; this could help decide whether the pillar was caused by pencil or plate crystals. During airplane flights, watch for the subsun; when the simplest form of snow—not flakes but individual crystals—falls, look for the sunstreak. Finally, watch for the fairly rare "double sun", and try to learn if it is a part of a pillar.

Sun pillars are vertical columns of light which may sometimes be visible extending up from or (more rarely) down from the Sun when the Sun is low in the sky. Most of them are caused by *plate crystals* of ice floating nearly horizontally and reflecting the Sun. Robert Greenler and colleagues discovered by computer simulations that pillars that occur with the Sun when it is much higher in the sky (10 or even 20 degrees) must be explained by *pencil crystals* of ice making the reflection. In any case, the fact that refraction is not involved in producing the sun pillars prevents them from having their own color—though they often do take on the gold, orange, or red of the low Sun.

Measure the length of sun pillars; rarely, they may extend for up to 15 degrees or more! You should also record the elevation of the Sun (which helps determine what their appearance will be like)—or, if the Sun is below the horizon from the observer's viewpoint, the exact time and date (so the Sun's position can be calculated).

If a sun pillar is seen when the Sun is 10 degrees or more high, then we can assume it was caused by a pencil crystal. But a sun pillar observed when the Sun is much lower could be caused by either kind of crystal. The way to tell the difference is to note other halo phenomena visible at the same time. The halo effect which often accompanies pillars caused by pencil crystals is the *upper tangential arc,* part of the circumscribed halo. (See Activity 82.) If this arc and the pillar remain visible for a while and other halo phenomena (particularly mock suns) are not, you may conclude that pencil crystals were responsible.

Airplane flights are usually not free (and our Activities are supposed to be no-cost), but if you are on an airplane, you should seize the opportunity to look for the form a sun pillar takes when it is caused by ice crystals reflecting up to you from far below the Sun. This *subsun* appears as a sometimes brilliant elliptical spot of light (sometimes reported as a UFO!) seen directly beneath the Sun as far below the horizon as the Sun is above. You may see a subsun from a hill if enough ice crystals are floating near ground level as the simplest form of snow. You are more likely, when such snow occurs and the Sun is out, to see a *sunstreak*—the name given to a sun pillar extending down from the Sun not in the sky but actually in front of distant landscape (usually hills). For more on this snow and the halo effects it produces, see the next activity.

Finally, there is a mysterious sky phenomenon that may be best explained as a form of sun pillar—the *double sun.* (See Activity 48 for an illustration.) Sometimes there appears to be a surprisingly convincing duplicate of the Sun just above it. Minnaert mentions rare cases when the duplicate is below and when two or even three duplicates have been seen. But he also states, "Probably this phenomenon is simply due to a local enhancing of the brightness of the pillar of light by unequal distribution of clouds." I am not so sure. Watch for the double sun and sketch or photograph it, noting all relevant information.

Questions

1. How frequently can you see sun pillars? When you see one, how long is it and what is the altitude of the Sun at different stages during the period in which the pillar is visible?

2. What other halo phenomena (if any) are present, and can these help decide whether a low-sun pillar is caused by plate or pencil crystals? What is the longest

sun pillar you ever observed? The strongest? The highest Sun you ever see one with?

3. Can you spot a subsun from an airplane or a hill? What are its altitude (or "depression") below the horizon and the various aspects of its appearance? Can you spot a sunstreak when ice crystals occur in the air near ground level? What is the Sun's altitude when you see it? How close must the crystals causing the sunstreak be?

4. Can you observe the double sun? What are all aspects of its appearance, the Sun's altitude, and any other relevant details?

81.

Moon Pillars and Light Pillars

Look for moon pillars, noting comparable information about them as for sun pillars in the previous activity. Look for light pillars over streetlights and other light sources in the moderate distance. Measure the length of the light pillars, and try to identify the location of the light source causing them. See how the length of the pillars changes as you approach the light source.

The Sun is not the only light source that can produce pillars of light in ice crystals reflecting it—so can the Moon and even mundane or artificial lights.

Moon pillars can be observed fairly often (probably more than a few times a year to a persistent observer in most climates). Find out at how many of the moonrises or moonsets you watch you can see them. Of course, the Moon's phase is important; it would be interesting to learn the smallest phase that can produce a visible moon pillar. As with sun pillars, you should note the Moon's altitude and the length of the pillar and also whether any other halo phenomena are visible.

Stranger and far less often seen than moon pillars in most climates are *light pillars*—pillars of light caused by sources of radiance other than the Sun or Moon. Streetlights are most often the sources, and the pillars are best seen far enough from them so that many can be seen and, possibly, against a darker background. Within small towns, however, light pillars have been seen extending up to the zenith (an effect of perspective) and been mistaken for the vertical rays characteristic of certain auroral displays!

Like the aurora, light pillars are most often seen at rather high latitudes, but it is not extreme northerliness or southerliness that is the key. Light pillars are formed when there are enough ice crystals floating relatively near ground level. The crystals in this case are classified as a form of snow, a form likely to occur often only in rather cold climates. The United States above 40 degrees north is cold enough in winter for a number of displays; farther south it is cold enough much less often. Usually a falling unit of snow is a *flake* or even an *aggregate* of flakes. The simple ice crystal as snow is sometimes called *diamond dust,* no doubt due to its sparkling in sunlight (and sometimes forming a sunstreak as discussed in the previous activity) in the air on calm mornings that favor its occurrence. At night you might not see it (especially if it is not close to you), but you might detect its presence indirectly by sighting light pillars.

Questions

1. At how many moonrises and moonsets can you see moon pillars? What are the Moon's altitude and the length of the pillar(s)? Are any other halo phenomena visible? What are the longest moon pillar and the one from highest Moon that you can see? What is the smallest lunar phase at which you can see a moon pillar?

2. Can you see light pillars? How long are they? How long are they at various distances from the light sources causing them? Knowing that pillars take on the color of their light source and knowing the color of different kinds of artificial lighting (see Activity 60), can you tell which kind of light (mercury vapor, HPS, and so on) in the distance is causing a particular pillar?

82.

Circumscribed Halos

Look for traces of the circumscribed halo, bearing in mind the different appearances it takes at different altitudes of the Sun. Sketch (and photograph, if possible) what you see of it and any other halo phenomena occurring at the same time. Be sure to note the solar altitude.

Robert Greenler suggests that the *circumscribed halo* should more reasonably be called the *circumscribing halo* because it is the additional arcs of light around the 22-degree halo that we should have a specific name for, not the entire display of halo and arcs. Of course, there is already a weight of tradition behind the original term, so we have to think twice before trying to change it. But there is more than a variety of names to this phenomenon: There is also a variety of forms that can make identification of it bewildering unless you know just what to look for and when to look for it.

Figure 15 shows the predicted forms of the circumscribed halo at different solar elevations at which it may be seen. As you can see, at high solar elevations (40 to 70 degrees), the circumscribed halo looks like handles on either side of the 22-degree halo. (Note that, above about 70 degrees, the "handles" no longer extend beyond the 22-halo itself; no circumscribed halo is visible.) Remember that you might see only part of the arcs or only part may be prominent so that you need to know where to look at that elevation of the Sun for fainter parts that will complete the figure. (By the way, the 22-degree halo itself usually is, but need not be, visible during a display of the circumscribed halo.)

Between 40 and 30 degrees solar altitude, there is a dramatic change, as the "handles" break and their lower parts dwindle to a more strongly downward curving arc. Since this lower arc is now near the hazy horizon, it is less likely to be seen. But the upper section of the handles remains prominent and becomes known as the *upper tangential arc*—sometimes seen spectacularly even when the 22-degree halo is not, and sometimes seen just above the top end of a long sun pillar near sunset.

Some form of the circumscribed halo is visible rather often; find out how often in your climate. But once in a while what looks a lot like parts of the circumscribed halo may actually be the rather rare arcs of Parry or Lowitz. Readers interested in learning the distinctions can refer to Greenler's *Rainbows, Halos, and Glories*.

But are the predicted forms of the circumscribed halo at different altitudes precisely correct, precisely what an observer would see when the phenomenon is fully developed? They probably are for this rather common—albeit complex and

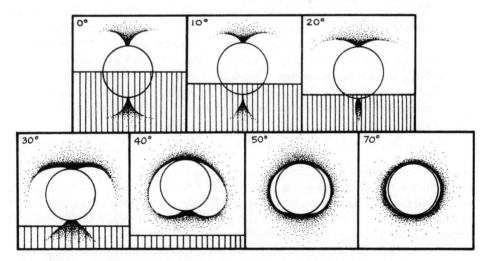

Figure 15 Forms of the circumscribed halo at different altitudes of the Sun (or Moon).

many-faced—phenomenon. But to be sure, one should always sketch and photograph the circumscribed halo carefully and make careful notes about just what was seen. The possibility of thereby detecting a Parry arc, Lowitz arc, or even a previously unknown halo phenomenon is also increased.

Questions

1. How often do you see some part of the circumscribed halo? How often do you see all of the phenomenon that can be visible at that particular sun elevation?

2. How many of the different forms (at different solar elevations) have you seen? What is the longest-lasting display? Can you watch a display go through the remarkable transition between 40 and 30 degrees solar altitude?

3. What is the exact form of the phenomenon you see? Might it be an effect other than the circumscribed halo (even a previously unknown one)? Do you see any other halo phenomena you know during the display?

83.

Circumzenithal Arc and Circumhorizontal Arc

When the Sun is less than 32 degrees high and cirrus clouds are present far above the Sun, look for the circumzenithal arc. Note the sun's altitude and the arc's altitude. Estimate its length, and record the colors it displays (including which colors are most prominent). Notice what other halo phenomena are visible at the time of the display. When the Sun is more than 58 degrees high and cirrus clouds are present far below the Sun, look for the circumhorizontal arc.

Some observers think the *circumzenithal arc* is the most beautiful of all halo phenomena. As its name suggests, it is an arc of a circle that would have the zenith (overhead point) at its (the circle's) center. What the name does not suggest is that this arc often shows all the colors of the rainbow and with great saturation and intensity. If long enough at its altitude, the arc also seems to have a gentle curve so that it looks like—in fact, is sometimes mistaken for—an upside-down rainbow.

The circumzenithal arc is probably visible at least a few times a year to most reasonably dedicated observers who know where to look. (Find out, however, how often in a year you can see it.) Of course, where to look is the problem for the average person: The arc always forms very high in the sky above the Sun, a place where very few people look often unless they have specific reason to. There is also a special time for visibility of this arc. Like all halo phenomena, it occurs when there are the proper ice crystals in the proper orientations in the thin, feathery cirrus (or cirrostratus) clouds. But it is also true that it can occur only when the Sun is less than 32 degrees altitude—an even stricter limitation in this respect than that of the rainbow.

The circumzenithal arc can extend as much as, or almost as much as, one-third of the way around the entire sky at its altitude. Of course, that altitude is always rather high (it is always a little more than 46 degrees above the Sun), so one-third of the way around the sky is not as long as it might sound.

There is, however, the halo phenomenon that complements the circum-zenithal arc—the *circumhorizontal arc* (caused by the same ray path except heading down out of the crystals). This arc can also be almost one-third of the way around the sky at its altitude—an altitude that is never less than about 46 degrees below the Sun. So this also bright and fully colored phenomenon can be longer (and wider) than a rainbow! Alas that the full display must be very rare for several reasons. For one thing, it would require the right kind of clouds to be covering a lot of the sky. Also, the circumhorizontal arc can only appear when the Sun is higher than 58 degrees. (Ninety degrees—at zenith—minus 32—the circumzenithal arc's extreme altitude of formation—equals 58.) Thus people at the latitudes of the United States and Europe can only hope to see the circumhorizontal arc around the noontime hours of the few months around the summer solstice.

Questions

1. How often can you see the circumzenithal arc? What is the Sun's altitude when you spot it? How long is the arc? How prominent is it? How many colors are visible in it? What other halo phenomena are seen?

2. How often do you see the circumhorizontal arc? What is the Sun's altitude and the arc's length, prominence, and colors? What other halo phenomena are visible with it?

84.

Rarer Halo Phenomena

When cirrus clouds cover large sections of the sky, look for more uncommon halo phenomena like the 46-degree halo, halos of unusual radius, the parhelic circle, the anthelion, and the paranthelia. If you see any of them, describe the appearance carefully, and note all pertinent aspects of the observation— especially the Sun's altitude and whatever other halo phenomena are visible at the time.

Each year, an alert observer who knows where to look may spot parts of the 22-degree halo and mock suns dozens of times. But there are many halo phenomena that are far less common.

Figure 16 shows a sampling of these. One of the most interesting phenomena is the *46-degree halo.* This is the *large halo* that makes the huge 22-degree halo seem small. Unfortunately, the 46-degree halo is rarely, if ever, seen in its entirety. It arises from light taking a different path through ice crystals than for the 22-degree halo and, in this respect, is related to the circumzenithal arc; but the arc seems to be seen far more often than sections of the 46-degree halo.

There have been reliable observations of *halos of unusual radius:* About 8-, 18-,

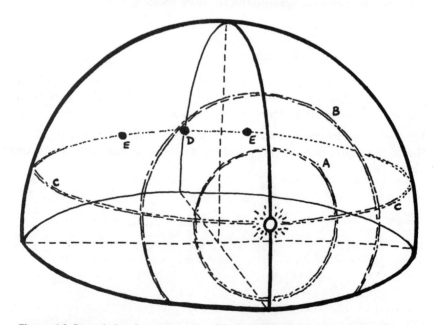

Figure 16 Rarer halo phenomena: A—22-degree halo (common); B—46-degree halo; C—parhelic circle; D—anthelion; E—paranthelia (should be shown further to either side of D).

20-, and 35-degree radii have been reported a number of times; once, up to six halos were seen at one time! They are rare, but do look for them when cirri are widespread and other halo phenomena seen.

Another remarkable halo effect is the *parhelic circle*. It goes around the entire sky at the height of the parhelia (mock suns), thus, also, at the height of the Sun. Usually only part of it is seen. Unlike the 22-degree halo, the parhelic circle is only a reflection effect, showing no color. What it may show are several concentrations of light along it. On the exact opposite side of the sky from the Sun (but at the same altitude) is the *anthelion;* 120 degrees of azimuth to either side of the Sun (60 degrees to either side of anthelion) on the parhelic circle are the *paranthelia.*

All procedures that apply to recording observations of more common halo effects apply to sightings of these. But a good observation of the rarer halo phenomena could greatly aid our understanding of them. And discovering a new halo effect is not out of the question!

Questions

1. Can you see any of the 46-degree halo or halos of unusual radius? What are the Sun's altitude, other halo phenomena, and the sky and meteorological conditions at the time of the sighting?

2. Can you see all or part of the parhelic circle? How about the much rarer anthelion or paranthelia on it? Can you record all of the relevant information about them and the conditions during the sighting?

85.

Coronas

Observe coronas around the Moon and (usually reflected in water or glass) around the Sun. Measure the radius of the first red ring of the corona and also any farther-out ones. Note the colors and how many red rings are visible. Try to determine by the radii of the red rings whether the corona is being caused by cloud droplets or ice needles. Study the size and prominence of entoptic coronas, trying to relate these to other measures of your eye's tiredness.

When some people see around the cloud-surrounded Moon a small disk of blue or green bounded by a red band they call it a halo. But we have seen in the preceding activities that halos are far larger and otherwise different. The vivid disk and band of colors around the Moon—and Sun—are called a *corona* (not to be confused with the corona that is the outer atmosphere of the Sun visible during total solar eclipses).

Coronas are caused by tiny cloud droplets or ice needles close enough to the wavelengths of visible light to produce an *interference* pattern. The explanation of this process is given in Activity 73.

The first set of colors—often the only set—in a corona is the disk of blue or green light nearest the Moon (or Sun) and the band of red light, which bounds it. The radius of the circle bounded by this (first) red band might typically be anywhere from 0.5 degree to 3.0 degrees or more. In good displays, a second, or even a third, fourth, and fifth red band can be spotted at greater distances. The final red band in one of these superb displays might be 5.0, 10.0, or (very rarely) even more degrees from the Moon or Sun. If you should notice that the radius of the first set of colors is not a little larger than the farther-out ones, but is of precisely the same radius, then you are probably observing a corona caused by ice needles. An easier rule of thumb to remember is that the larger the sets of colors are, the smaller the droplets (or thinner the ice needles) causing the display.

In each corona, you should measure the distances out to each of the red bands. You should try to identify the type of cloud causing the display. And you should also record the colors: If they are rather weak, the droplets must be of many sizes; if pastels, then the droplet sizes are more nearly the same; and if pure, then the droplets are of unusually uniform size.

Coronas occur much more frequently with the Sun (indeed with almost any kind of cloud that is not thick enough to completely hide the Sun). But the clouds are rendered so bright near the Sun that direct viewing of them there is seldom possible (or advisable). The best solution to this is to look at the reflection of the Sun and clouds in calm water. A sky-wonder otherwise missed can be perceived by gazing into even the humblest of rainwater puddles!

Our next activity is devoted to those lovely sections and fragments of coronas called iridescent clouds. But there is a special kind of corona you can observe even when there are no clouds, no Sun, and no Moon. This is an *entoptic corona*. When you look at a streetlight—or any bright light source against a fairly dark background—you may see a corona that arises within the eye itself! Entoptic coronas are caused by tiny irregularities of the peripheral lens and the cornea surface producing the interference pattern. Fatigued eyes make entoptic coronas larger and more prominent. Study these coronas and try to find a way of correlating their size and prominence to some other measure of how tired (focusing muscles overworked?) your eyes are. How can you tell an entoptic corona from one caused by thin mist or fog (perhaps scarcely visible) around a streetlight? Block the light source, and you still see a fog- (or cloud-) caused corona—but not an entoptic corona.

Questions

1. What is the angular radius of each set of colors you see in a corona? Exactly what are the colors and how pure are they? Can you identify the causative clouds?

How many sets of colors are there? What is the largest corona you ever see? What is the one with the most red rings? Can you tell by the relative size of the sets of colors whether the corona is probably caused by cloud droplets or by ice needles?

2. How large and prominent are entoptic coronas when your eyes are tired? When your eyes are rested? What other measure of your eyes' tiredness can you correlate with these features of entoptic coronas?

86.

Iridescent Clouds

Look for iridescent clouds near the Moon and near the reflected image of the Sun. Look also for iridescence on clouds far from the Sun, making special note of its angular distance from the Sun. Notice the distribution of colors in iridescent clouds, and try to determine to what extent it is the result of angular distance from the Sun to what extent position in cloud due to size of cloud droplets.

In your observations of coronas with the Sun and Moon, you will often find that only sections or patches of the corona bands are visible—in which case they are called *iridescent clouds*.

The most fascinating thing is that, when iridescent clouds occur at larger angular distances from the Sun (or Moon), their distribution is found to follow the contours of the clouds more than where the positioning would be expected in the corona. In such a situation, it is the size of the droplets that becomes more important than the angular distance from the Sun; so, for instance, the smaller droplets at the edges of clouds will generally be of a different color (red or blue-green) than the thicker central regions of the clouds.

Occasionally you can see iridescent clouds of quite prominent colors very far from the Sun: On a small number of occasions, I have spotted them at distances of 40 to 60 degrees away from the Sun. Measure how far out the ones you see are, and, of course, note the distribution of colors.

A special kind of iridescent cloud is *nacreous clouds,* also known as *mother-of-pearl clouds.* These rare clouds are the second highest of all kinds. (Only noctilucent clouds, discussed in Activity 96, are higher.) Unlike noctilucent clouds, they have been seen at low latitudes. Nacreous clouds are extremely cold because they are located between about 12 to 20 miles up. These clouds, which show the finest of all iridescence, are only visible when the Sun is low or actually below the horizon.

Questions

1. What are the colors and distribution of colors in iridescent clouds you observe? How far from the Sun can you ever spot iridescence?

2. Can you observe nacreous clouds? Can you note both their altitude and the Sun's altitude, the distribution of their colors, and any meteorological conditions that pertain to them?

87.

Glories

Try to observe the glory on clouds, on your next airplane flight, or at the center of the circle formed by a fogbow. Note the colors, and measure the angular distance to each of the red bands. Try to identify the causative clouds. Observe whether the central areas of the glory (around any shadow, if present) is dark or bright.

Before airplane flights, it was usually only in mountainous regions that an observer would chance to see—crowning the head of his or her distorted, elongated, conical shadow—an archery-target-like display of alternating rings of blue or green and red. The shadow with this crown was called *the Spectre of the Brocken* (the Brocken being the highest peak in the Harz Mountains of central Germany). But the crown of rings of color, now so frequently visible from airplanes, is called the *glory*.

Glories might be thought of as coronas (see Activity 85) occurring around the light backscattered from cloud (or fog) droplets at the anti-solar point. In reality, the size of their rings and other features do not quite conform with this idea of them as an *anti-corona*. In fact, although purely mathematical treatments of the glory exist, no suitable physical model yet exists. Perhaps your own observations can help provide some clues.

Airplane flights are usually not free, but when you happen to take one, chances are good that, at some point, you can spot a glory on clouds below. If the plane is near enough to the clouds, you can see its shadow with the glory surrounding it. You can even notice that the exact center of the glory corresponds to your position on the plane.

To see a glory in thick fog, a rising Sun or, at night, car headlights—any bright light source behind you—can suffice. Minnaert points out that the glory always somehow looks closer than the fogbow in these situations—even though this is not the case.

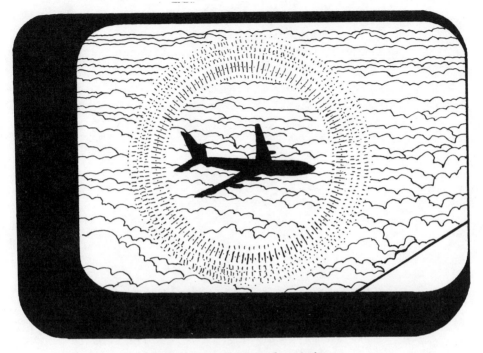

A glory and a shadow of an airplane.

Wherever you see the glory, you should note its colors and determine the angular radius of each of the red rings. There may be several rings visible; as with the corona, five seems to be the record. If you can determine the type of clouds (with water droplets or ice needles?) causing the display, that is important information to record. Also notice if the central area of the glory (the part around the plane's shadow or your head's shadow if these are visible) is bright or dark. The existence of bright-centered and dark-centered glories is supposedly one of the troublesome points for their explanation. Perhaps more data on this will help.

Questions

1. Can you see a glory on your next airplane flight? With Sun, streetlight, or car headlights behind you in the fog? What are the colors and the angular distance to each of the reddish rings?

2. Do you see the shadow of your airplane in a glory? Is a glory you see bright or dark in its center (around any shadow, if present)?

ECLIPSES

88.

First and Last Naked-Eye Visibility of Earth's Penumbra and Umbra

Watch for the first and last visibility of the Earth's penumbra on the Moon during a lunar eclipse. Record the times you first suspect and first are certain you are seeing this subtle shading. Do the same things for the first and last naked-eye visibility of the Earth's umbra.

During an eclipse of the Moon, the Earth moves between Sun and Moon, casting its shadow on the latter. But like all shadows, the Earth's actually consists of two parts: the central, darker *umbra,* and the peripheral, less dark *penumbra.*

Figure 17(a) shows the Moon's path through the cross-section of the penumbra and umbra projected on the sky. Figure 17(b) shows the view from space of the Sun, Earth, and Moon. In the second diagram, it can be seen that a viewer (or a Moon) anywhere within the umbra would have the Sun completely blocked from sight by the Earth. A viewer (or a Moon) anywhere in the penumbra would have the Sun partly blocked from view by the penumbra.

At every total lunar eclipse, the Moon goes through all of the stages on our diagrams. At a partial lunar eclipse, only part of the Moon passes through the edge of the umbra. At a *penumbral lunar eclipse,* the Moon skims only through penumbra.

One final point needs to be understood. Sunlight gets refracted by Earth's atmosphere into the umbra so that the umbra is rarely completely dark: The Moon dims tremendously during total eclipse but usually does not disappear completely due to this typically reddened sunlight. However, generally, the deeper into the penumbra or umbra the Moon goes, the darker it gets. Also, cloudiness in Earth's lower atmosphere and volcanic ash or aerosol in the higher atmosphere can darken umbra and penumbra. All of this means that different parts of the umbra and penumbra will be of different darkness at every eclipse and that observations of the Moon passing through these parts can tell us a lot about the shadow and the regions of Earth's atmosphere affecting them. Most of us who love the beauty of lunar eclipses also want to know all the particulars that went into making them look the way they do, anyway.

How can we learn such particulars? The next two activities concern the colors and brightness of the Moon during total lunar eclipses, famous topics about which I hope to present a few fresh details. But the main part of our current activity, however, is one that has been almost entirely neglected, yet also provides information. I refer to studying penumbral eclipses of the Moon or the penumbral

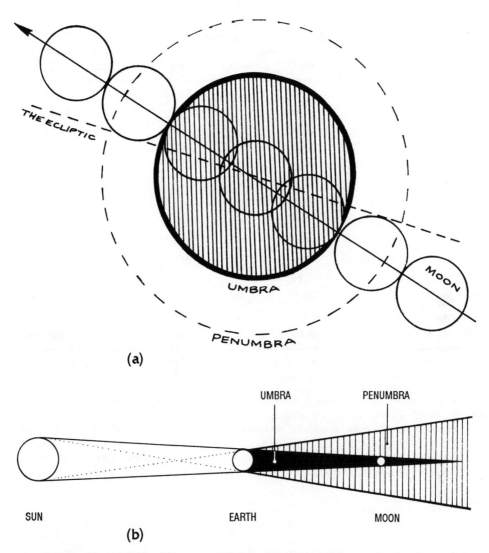

Figure 17 (a) Lunar eclipse in the sky with cross-section of Earth's shadow; (b) Lunar eclipse in space (sizes and distances not to scale).

parts of partial and total lunar eclipses. (See Table 16 for a list of all soon-upcoming lunar eclipses—including penumbral.)

The simplest and most straightforward penumbra project is to note the time when you can first and last see any trace of penumbral shading on the Moon. Remember that when the Moon first enters the penumbra it is entering the most peripheral, lightest portion of it, and the penumbra will not be detectable. The value usually quoted for when penumbral shading is first visible at the Moon's edge

175

Table 16
All lunar eclipses, 1990–95*

Date	Time§	Mag**	Dir§§	DurUmb***	DurTot§§§	Type
1990 Feb 9	19:13	1.07	S	204	42	Total
1990 Aug 6	14:12	0.68	N	176	—	Partial
1991 Jan 30	6:00	(0.88)	S	—	—	Penumbral
1991 Jun 27	3:16	(0.31)	S	—	—	Penumbral
1991 Jul 26	18:09	(0.25)	N	—	—	Penumbral
1991 Dec 21	10:34	0.09	N	64	—	Partial
1992 Jun 15	4:58	0.68	S	180	—	Partial
1992 Dec 9	23:45	1.27	N	208	74	Total
1993 Jun 4	13:02	1.56	N	218	96	Total
1993 Nov 29	6:26	1.09	S	210	46	Total
1994 May 25	3:32	0.24	N	104	—	Partial
1994 Nov 18	6:45	(0.88)	S	—	—	Penumbral
1995 Apr 15	12:19	0.11	S	78	—	Partial
1995 Oct 8	16:05	(0.83)	N	—	—	Penumbral

* Data from Jean Meeus, *Astronomical Tables of the Sun, Moon, and Planets*

§ Ephemeris Time, which for these purposes is virtually identical to universal Time (see "Note on the Measurement of Time, Position, Angular Distances, and Brightnesses in Astronomy"). The time given is for mideclipse; if it falls during the night for your location, the eclipse is visible from your area

** "Magnitude" of eclipse—not brightness here, but the percentage of the Moon's diameter covered with umbra or (if in parentheses) penumbra at maximum eclipse, 1.00 (100%) or more is total; "1.07" means the Moon is 1.07 times its own diameter inside umbra

§§ Direction of Moon from center of umbra at mideclipse (*N* means north of umbra center, *S,* south)

*** Duration in minutes of umbral eclipse (that is, eclipse during which at least some part of the Moon is in the umbra)

§§§ Duration of total eclipse

is when the Moon is about 50 percent of the way into the penumbra. That figure may be conservative, however. At the very least, it is only an average, so that, at dark, eclipses, shading can be seen with the Moon much less farther in.

Detecting the penumbra is usually best done with the naked eye. And, unlike almost any other kind of astronomical observing, it may be better for your eyes not to be dark-adapted to see the penumbra; you may detect it more easily if you have just come out from a lighted room.

What about noting the time when the umbra is first visible to the naked eye? This ends up being more a test of the eye's resolving power than anything else. The umbra should always be dark enough in relation to the rest of the Moon for its presence to be detected with the unaided eye not long after its first tiny trace is glimpsed in a telescope.

Questions

1. When can you first and last detect penumbral shading on the Moon during an eclipse? Does it correspond well with how dark the total eclipse is? Do you notice any odd variations in the penumbra's shading?
2. When can you first and last detect umbra on the Moon with the naked eye?

89.

Colors at a Lunar Eclipse

With the naked eye, study the colors and shadings on the Moon at a total lunar eclipse or a large partial eclipse. Sketch their distribution at least every few minutes and more often when justified.

We often hear it suggested that observers note the overall color of the totally eclipsed Moon—to help determine the Danjon rating (see the next activity), which is really primarily aimed at judging how dark an eclipse is. Anyone who has watched more than a few minutes of a total eclipse of the Moon, however, knows well that the eclipsed lunar disk usually gives an ever-changing display of different shades and hues. This is not to say that one cannot often characterize an eclipse as being generally dark red, orange, or gray, but there are many details of component or auxiliary hues and shadings to be noted.

You might suppose that such details would be best studied with a telescope. In reality, there are some areas of color that magnifying only will spread out too much and weaken. Eclipse observations with naked eye, binoculars, and telescopes all nicely complement one another.

The times when the most hues and shadings are seen might often be near the edge of the umbra, so it is at the times when this edge is on the Moon that you may find yourself making new sketches of what you are seeing every minute or so! Minnaert writes of "bright sea-green, pale golden, copper, peach-blossom pink" in the outer part of the shadow (by which he certainly means the outer part of the umbra). There is, at a lunar eclipse, no easy replacement for what the eye and a sketch pad can show. No photographs will ever catch all the subtleties of this kind.

Nor is total eclipse the time to start looking for them. There comes a time during the partial phase of a total eclipse—or during a large partial eclipse—when color and shading of light and dark becomes visible in the part of the Moon already covered by the umbra. Note the time (is it different after totality than before?) and what is seen.

Questions

1. When do you first, with the naked eye, see color in the umbra during a lunar eclipse? When do you last see it? How does the identity of the color and the earliness (or lateness) of its first appearance correlate with the color and brightness of the total part of the eclipse?

2. What are the hues and shadings of bright and dark, and what is the pattern of their distribution on the Moon during a total lunar eclipse? Can you put your sketches together to make a map of all that part of the umbra that the Moon passed through during the eclipse?

90.

Brightness of the Eclipsed Moon

Rate the totally eclipsed Moon's brightness by color and other features on the Danjon scale. If you are nearsighted, take off your glasses and compare the out-of-focus Moon to out-of-focus stars of known brightness. If you have binoculars, look through the large end at the Moon and, after applying a brightness correction, compare its brightness to stars seen with the naked eye. Note visibility of the Moon's edge and how faint of stars become visible at each stage of the partial eclipse.

The full Moon's usual brightness of about magnitude $-12\frac{1}{2}$ dims to roughly magnitude -4 at a bright total lunar eclipse, and roughly magnitude $+4.0$ at a very dark one. In recent decades, the traditional approach has been to rate a total lunar eclipse's brightness on the scale designed by A. Danjon. This scale offers five major levels of L (luminosity), each with its own definition. (See Table 17.)

The scale is extremely useful. There are, however, many eclipses that seem to be hybrids. In these cases, you can sometimes suggest a fraction between two ratings or even give separate ratings to different parts of the Moon (corresponding to different lateral strips of the umbra). And what about different stages of the total eclipse? Books often maintain that the Danjon rating should ideally be made around the time of midtotality. But the Danjon descriptions do include some comments about the edge of the umbra, which the Moon might only sample early and late in totality.

Perhaps the best adjunct to the Danjon rating is to compare the eclipsed Moon's brightness with that of planets or stars. But of course the Moon's total light

Table 17
Danjon's brightness scale for total lunar eclipses (L stands for luminosity)

L = 0	Very dark eclipse; Moon hardly visible, especially near midtotality
L = 1	Dark eclipse; gray-to-brown coloring; details on the disk hardly discernible
L = 2	Dark red or rust-colored eclipse with dark area in the center of shadow, the edge brighter
L = 3	Brick red eclipse, the shadow often bordered with a brighter yellow edge
L = 4	Orange or copper-colored, very bright eclipse with bright bluish edge

is spread over a far larger area ... how can we compare the total magnitudes of such different objects?

If you wear rather strong glasses for nearsightedness, you need only take them off to find the Moon and stars reduced to out-of-focus images of roughly similar size so that they can be compared. (Remember atmospheric extinction [see Table 3] if the Moon is low or a comparison star is at a very different altitude.) If you do not wear glasses, you can try comparing Moon and stars in a reflective object like a Christmas tree ornament (which makes the Moon look tiny)!

Suppose the Moon is brighter than any star? If you have binoculars, you can gaze at the Moon through the large end to make it look like a greatly dimmed point of light that you can then compare to stars seen with the naked eye. Only the magnification of the binoculars affects how dimmed the Moon, seen the "wrong" way through them, will be. Assuming 25 percent light loss in the optics, the Association of Lunar and Planetary Observers gives these figures for different magnifications: 6X—4.2 magnitudes dimmer; 7X—4.5; 8X—4.8; 10X—5.3; 11X—5.5; 20X—6.8.

How else can we abet the Danjon rating? A few of the Danjon descriptions do mention visibility of markings of the Moon. See if you can add to the other descriptions by noting how much more or less visible the lunar seas are at such eclipses. (What is the smallest sea seen?) What about visibility of the Moon's edge? This is tricky because the brightness of one side of the Moon in eclipse may make the edge of the other side seem less visible.

Finally, a further measure of eclipse darkness is the glorious emergence of numerous stars during the eclipse. Even the brightest eclipse should permit this effect roughly as well as the darkest. Only a greater visibility of stars during an early partial phase might suggest a much darker eclipse—and even this might be difficult to ascertain with quick limiting magnitude tests. Moreover, one would have to take the natural limiting magnitude at that site (perhaps affected by light pollution) and the transparency that night into account.

Indeed, all ratings of the Moon's brightness and colors during an eclipse are subject to some variability according to your weather and sky conditions. Try to pick a site far from city lights and hope for very clear skies!

Questions

1. What is your Danjon rating for a total lunar eclipse you see? Is a whole-number rating sufficient? Do you need different ratings for different parts of the Moon or for different parts of the total eclipse?

2. Can you estimate the magnitude of the totally eclipsed Moon by comparison with stars or planets by using the methods involving glasses, binoculars, or reflective objects?

3. What other details can you use as measures of eclipse brightness? At what stages in partial phases (or at a partial eclipse) do various levels of improvement in limiting magnitude of stars occur?

91.

Sun-Pictures During a Partial Solar Eclipse

Study sun-pictures and shadows during a partial eclipse of the Sun or during the partial phases of a total eclipse of the Sun.

Without special filters and full knowledge of exactly what you are doing, you must not look directly at the Sun during a partial solar eclipse. On the other hand, projecting an image of the Sun to observe is easy and can be quite safe.

Unless the image is projected by binoculars or telescope, it is unlikely to show any such detail as sunspots. But a piece of cardboard with a pinhole in it is sufficient to show a tiny sun-picture (projected image of the Sun) revealing how much of the Sun has been blocked off by the Moon during a solar eclipse. You need only hold the cardboard roughly perpendicular to the rays of the Sun—itself behind you— and look for the sun-picture on any suitable "screen" (another piece of cardboard?). The distance at which a sharp image of given size is formed depends on the size of the pinhole, but it is easy to move your cardboard (or "screen") to adjust and find the proper distance.

It is less well known that the chinks between leaves on trees can form remarkable sun-pictures, too. Of course, the line-up of Sun, chink, and ground will seldom be such as to cause circular images. You will find the sunlight dappling the shade under trees to be an assortment of elliptical sun-pictures of different size, sharpness, and brightness. I have never seen a photo showing a throng of these

Sun-pictures during a partial solar eclipse.

shadows with "bites" taken out of them all by the Moon during a solar eclipse! Try to take such a photograph, or at least observe this marvelous sight.

Not just sun-pictures but the shadows cast by the Sun are affected by a partial solar eclipse. Certainly the color of the shadows should change with the changing color of sunlight and sky. (See the next activity.) But the shape changes, too. The biggest question is how soon this is noticeable. When the eclipse is nearly total, the crescent Sun causes objects to cast strangely curved shadows. You could photograph or trace around a shadow on paper as an eclipse begins, then again at different stages of the partial eclipse to see when change was first noticeable.

(For a list of upcoming solar eclipses, see Table 18.)

Questions

1. Can you use a pinhole in cardboard to cast a small sun-picture showing the stages of a solar eclipse? Can you identify the Moon's form in sun-pictures in the dappled sunlight under trees?

2. Can you detect a change in the color and shape of shadows during partial solar eclipse? When is the change in shape first noted?

92.

Darkening and Color of the Sky During a Partial Solar Eclipse

Observe the darkening of the sky and landscape during the progress of a solar eclipse. Note also the change in the color of sunlight.

As more and more of the Sun is covered during an eclipse, the sky and landscape darken and change color. The trick is to find interesting ways to show these changes dramatically.

If you are accustomed to measuring the darkness/blueness of the blue sky (see Activities 56 and 57), your cardboard cyanometer or mental cyanometer will help you in this way note the change in the sky's brightness early and precisely during the eclipse. Observe and note the cyanometric changes in all parts of the sky. A camera's light meter is another way to follow these changes. And a series of photographs of sky and landscape (ideally with same f-number setting and exposure) makes a striking record of the changes for other people to see later.

It would be interesting to see when various people first think they can detect a darkening of the day during an eclipse. (I have never read an account of this being tested.) Then, of course, there is the behavior of plants and animals. Can you prove special activity of animals caused by the darkening environment long before totality? By camera light meter or other means, try to equate the intensity of overall illumination or of certain parts of the sky with that which occurs with various amounts of cloudiness on a non-eclipse day. How is a partial eclipse's darkening different than that on a day of increasing cloudiness?

One difference is in the change in the color of the sky. At some point in the eclipse, this factor may begin to confuse your efforts to rate the darkness of the sky by studying its blueness. The color of the sky and landscape change during a solar eclipse due to the part of the Sun whose light is predominating. The edges of the Sun are dimmer and redder, because from there we are receiving light from more grazing along the solar surface. It really may not be until about 70 percent of the Sun's diameter is covered that this light predominates enough to make a noticeable color change. But possibly a change could be detected sooner. See what you notice.

Questions

1. Can you measure the darkening of different parts of the sky during a partial solar eclipse (or partial phase of a total solar eclipse) by cyanometric study? By your camera's light meter? By a series of photographs?

2. How soon can various people detect the darkening? What is the average? Can you prove that animals act differently beginning at a certain stage in a solar eclipse? What stage is that?

3. How does the color of the sky change during an eclipse? At what point in the eclipse does this become noticeable?

93.

Eclipse and Noneclipse Shadow Bands

Look for shadow bands when the Sun is mostly covered by the Moon. Note at what stage in the eclipse they occur. Note also how wide each is, how far apart they are, and over how large an area you can see them. Estimate how fast they are moving and in what direction. Try to learn which way and with what velocity the surface winds and higher-altitude winds are blowing and other possibly pertinent facts about the weather. When no eclipse is in progress, try seeing shadow bands by Minnaert's experiment with bright planets and stars or by the light of approaching cars on a country road after a hot day.

Within just a few minutes before the start of totality (or within a few minutes after the end of totality) at a solar eclipse, an observer may sometimes—not always—see the eerie phenomenon known as *shadow bands*. Narrow strips of shadow not very far apart move, usually, at not too many miles per hour, across the ground and other surfaces, and sometimes across quite huge areas. An observer might increase his or her chances of seeing these sometimes rather indistinct bands by scanning a light-colored area of ground frequently in the key minutes.

There can no longer be any doubt that eclipse shadow bands are caused by unevenness in the distribution of light when the last thin crescent of the Sun *twinkles!* As in the case with twinkling of stars and seeing (see Activity 26), the winds causing shadow bands may be low or high altitude, but are probably most often rather high altitude.

Be on the lookout for shadow bands even many minutes before totality (and after totality), for there are a few cases of them occurring with more than a wire-thin Sun. But if you do not have an eclipse handy, you still can see essentially the same phenomenon in other ways—even if not on the grand scale of the eclipse version.

One other kind of shadow band must be extremely difficult to detect,

Table 18
Solar eclipses*

TOTAL AND ANNULAR, 1990-1996

Date	Time§	Maximum Duration** (minutes, seconds)	Type	Area of Visibility**
1990 Jan 26	20	2, 6	Annular	S. Atlantic, Antarctica
1990 Jul 22	3	2, 33	Total	Finland, N. and N.E. Siberia, N. Pacific
1991 Jan 15	24	7, 55	Annular	S.W. Australia, Tasmania, New Zealand, Pacific
1991 Jul 11	19	6, 54	Total	Pacific, Hawaii, Mexico, Central and S. America
1992 Jan 4	23	11, 42	Annular	Pacific
1992 Jun 30	12	5, 20	Total	Atlantic
1994 May 10	17	6, 14	Annular	E. Pacific, N. America, Atlantic, N.W. Africa
1994 Nov 3	14	4, 24	Total	S. America, S. Atlantic
1995 Apr 29	18	6, 38	Annular	Pacific, S. America
1995 Oct 24	5	2, 10	Total	Asia, Borneo, Pacific

(No total or annular eclipses in 1996)

PARTIAL, 1990-2003

Date	Time§	Maximum Magnitude§§
1992 Dec 24	1	0.84
1993 May 21	14	0.74
1993 Nov 13	22	0.93
1996 Apr 17	23	0.88
1996 Oct 12	14	0.76
1997 Sep 2	0	0.90
2000 Feb 5	13	0.58
2000 Jul 1	20	0.48
2000 Jul 31	2	0.60
2000 Dec 25	18	0.72

(No partial solar eclipses 2001-03.)

* Data derived from Jean Meeus, *Astronomical Tables of the Sun, Moon, and Planets*

§ Time of mideclipse, given in hours of Universal Time (see "Note on the Measurement of Time, Position, Angular Distances, and Brightnesses in Astronomy").

** Of the total or annular part of the eclipse

§§ Maximum "magnitude"—not brightness here, but fraction of Sun's diameter covered by Moon especially in today's world of so much light pollution, but it would be thrilling to observe. I refer to the shadow bands of twinkling bright stars and (though they usually twinkle little) bright planets. Minnaert suggests an extremely dark room that admits only the light of the bright planet or star we are using. Under ideal conditions, it ought to be possible to see dim shadow bands moving across the surface of a white sheet or other light-colored object you are using as a screen.

As Steve Albers once pointed out to me, there is a far more mundane but nonetheless interesting source of shadow bands. Your scene is a fairly dark country road at night after a day when the road was strongly heated. The distortion of the air due to rising heat waves will work its magic. On your screen—maybe a light-colored shirt you are wearing—shadow bands will run: the result of the twinkling light from distant car headlights.

Questions

1. Can you see shadow bands at a solar eclipse? How wide is each and how much space is between them? What is their orientation? Their speed and direction of motion? How long before or after totality are they seen?

2. By observing in a dark room admitting only the object's light, can you detect on a light-colored surface the shadow bands from a bright planet or star twinkling?

3. Can you detect shadow bands in the light from distant car headlights over a dark country road that was strongly heated by the Sun during the day? In which direction do they run?

94.

Some Auxiliary Phenomena of Total Solar Eclipses

During a total eclipse of the Sun, study not just the solar features but also the eclipse's effect on sky, landscape, weather, the apparent size of the Moon, animals and plants, and people.

There is even more to total solar eclipses than the awesome black Moon framed with the Sun's pearly *corona* (outer atmosphere).

Sometimes several minutes before totality, especially if light clouds are present, an observer can see the approach of the Moon's shadow in the sky. Try to spot it as long before (and after) totality as possible. When this mighty blue-gray or purple segment gets closer, the apparent speed of its climb up the sky increases greatly; when it reaches the Sun, darkness falls and total eclipse begins.

Weather changes before and during totality should be noted. Check the drop in temperature, and estimate the speed and direction of the famous *eclipse wind* if it occurs because of that drop. Notice what changes in clouds and cloud cover have occurred.

The degree of darkness varies a lot from one total solar eclipse to another. It is interesting to gather people's impressions (including your own) of how dark it seemed and compare these to more objective measures. Before the eclipse, know the position of planets and stars representing each magnitude and try—quickly— to see the faintest one you can detect. Observers who wore sunglasses during partial eclipse have seen stars as faint as fourth magnitude during total eclipse! Another measure of eclipse darkness is how fine a detail—for instance, print—you can make out even with the Sun's corona shining right on it.

Notice what parts of the sky at total eclipse are darkest; can you follow the shadow's progress during all of totality? At the eclipse in May 1984, John Bortle was able to detect the shadow even though it (or its central, umbral part) did not reach ground level where he was. If you ever find yourself not quite able to get to the zone of totality, you should still try looking for the darkened atmosphere in its direction. M. Minnaert even suggests that the Moon's shadow might be seen after sunset, when the total solar eclipse is occurring far beyond your horizon—passing through the layers of meteoroidal material that cause the zodiacal light. But what about simply seeing the shadow project through twilight glow?

The horizon during totality is often adorned with a thick band of deep orange or red light. Note its color, prominence, and width in all directions at various stages of the eclipse. It is all the light that, made red by distance, gets to you from atmosphere scores of miles away outside of the Moon's umbral shadow.

At the total solar eclipse on February 26, 1979, I noticed that the Moon seemed huge—far larger than at my previous total solar in 1970. The second eclipse was lower (but not at the horizon), its sky, cloudier. Note the size of the Moon at your next total solar eclipse and what factors might explain this odd version of the Moon Illusion. (See Activity 7.)

Will you find time and opportunity to notice changes in animals' behavior due to eclipse darkness? Proving cause and effect in these cases can be difficult. And then there is the effect on people: A tape recorder left running will be completely forgotten until after totality, when you can play back people's expressions (and your own expression) of wonder.

Questions

1. How long before and after totality can you detect the Moon's shadow in the distance? How does the distance at which the shadow is visible correlate with amount of cloudiness (and kinds of clouds)?

2. What changes in temperature, wind, cloud, and other weather conditions occur with the approach and then the onset of totality?

3. How dark does totality seem to different people? How dark does it seem at different total solar eclipses to people who have seen more than one? How dark does totality really get in terms of how faint of stars can be spotted and how fine of print can be read? (Make sure to take into account your amount of dark-adaptation prior to totality.)

4. How large does the Moon seem during total solar eclipse? What changes in fauna or flora that you notice do you think are demonstrably caused by the fall of eclipse darkness? What are the reactions of different people to the awesome experience of totality?

95.

Rainbows, Halos, and Cloud Coronas at Solar and Lunar Eclipses

Look for rainbows, halo phenomena, and cloud coronas during solar and lunar eclipses. Make careful notes about their time of occurrence and any unusual aspects of their appearance.

When discussing solar eclipses, the word *corona* will usually refer to the Sun's outermost atmosphere. But the dimmed Sun during partial or total solar eclipses can produce a set of interference colors formed in clouds such as those described in Activity 85—an effect also called a *corona*.

Rainbow, halo phenomena, and cloud coronas all can occur during solar and lunar eclipses and sometimes appear significantly different than usual.

Coronas caused by the Moon at a phase smaller than Full are sometimes seen to be asymmetrical due to the distribution of droplet sizes in the cloud—but other times due to the shape of the Moon. A mostly or totally eclipsed Moon is, unfortunately, only capable of producing weak coronas. But the smaller the remaining sliver of Sun at a solar eclipse gets, the more easily an observer may perceive a good cloud corona around it directly (still taking care not to look at the blinding Sun). And if such a corona is visible as we approach totality, we may be in for a magnificent sight: The solar corona (atmosphere of Sun), roughly bright as the Full Moon, should be capable of producing a rather good cloud corona, but this is not the magnificent sight I mean. What I refer to is the cloud corona caused by the *diamond,* the first or last speck of Sun's brilliant photosphere, which is often seen shining for a few seconds on its own through some valley on the edge of the Moon. That brightest of all starlike points of light you will ever see in the heavens is, because of its brightness and smallness, capable of producing the most exquisitely sharp cloud corona rings . . . as I have seen for myself. And I cannot help wondering if the famous *Baily's Beads*—multiple dots of Sun similar to but generally larger than the diamond—might make less observable but very striking multiple cloud coronas!

The differences in halo phenomena caused by eclipses might not be great, but they could be detectable—for instance, by a preponderance of red light in colorful halo effects like mock suns when they were caused by the redder light of the Sun's crescent. Might there be distortions of phenomena like sun pillars and the subsun near the time of totality? And the solar corona ought to be able to make at least dim halo effects.

Nobody wants to be clouded out or rained out of seeing an eclipse. But if the rain is moving off or seen in the distance, the eclipsed Sun can cause rainbows that can be very strange. I have heard of two cases of rainbows observed during total eclipses of the Sun. (They must occur far more often than this suggests, though.) In one case, the rainbow may have been caused by the eerie corona light. In the other case, the rainbow was apparently caused by the brief appearance (at start or end of totality) of the rather pink layer of Sun's atmosphere just lower than the corona, the *chromosphere.* I must admit that looking for rainbows during a total solar eclipse is treacherous because it means turning your gaze completely away from the main spectacle of the diamond, Baily's Beads, chromosphere, prominences, and solar corona. But if during the partial phases a rainbow has been visible, you are ready, and your quick glances may show you prodigies never before recorded.

Questions

1. Can you detect any halo phenomena, cloud coronas, or rainbows during the partial phases of a solar or lunar eclipse? Can you note any special differences between these phenomena and their noneclipse versions, such as differences in color or distortions in shape?

2. Can you glimpse a cloud corona around the diamond of a total solar eclipse or around each of multiple Baily's Beads? Halo effects caused by them? A rainbow caused by them or by the solar corona?

ELUSIVE GLOWS

96.

Noctilucent Clouds

If you are observing from at least 40 degrees north (preferably higher) latitude, search in the north sky during midtwilight for many weeks around summer solstice in hopes of spotting noctilucent clouds. Note their angular altitude (at precise times) and color, structure, and movement.

Five times higher than the tops of tall thunderstorms, in the coldest region of Earth's atmosphere, there sometimes appear the beautiful *noctilucent clouds*. So far they have never been observed further south in the northern hemisphere than about 42 degrees north, though a little farther south would be possible. Apparently it is only around summer solstice at these latitudes that the atmosphere 50 miles up is cold enough for the clouds.

The word *noctilucent* means "night-shining," though actually these clouds can shine no later than late twilight. The catch is that, at fairly high northern latitudes around the summer solstice, the twilight may technically last most or all "night" long. For, of course, the shining of noctilucent clouds is due to their being lit by the Sun and its afterglow—though long after the Sun has set at the surface, so that we, their observers, are in nearly full darkness.

Noctilucent clouds—called NLCs for short—occur at an altitude where floating micrometeoroids and the micrometeoritic remains of burned-up meteors are common. Rocket firings into noctilucent clouds have revealed that the clouds do indeed seem to be concentrations of this material, but coated with some ice. Noctilucent clouds need a lot more study, so careful observations and photos of them could be valuable to science.

Sometimes the glow of light pollution from a distant city to the north may be mistaken for dim noctilucent clouds. But the clouds are only visible when the Sun is between about 6 and 16 degrees below the horizon, and they often show beautiful color and structure. Noctilucent clouds are all silver-blue (unless also golden at the bottom). They show structure such as waves, billows, and even whirls, and they move at speeds of roughly 100 to 500 miles per hour! Of course, only very northerly observers will see the clouds at anything but great distance, so the angular motion should be slow. Needless to say, the motion can (and should) be tracked carefully nonetheless, as should any changes in the structure or color—and all of this with close attention to the time.

Questions

1. How often can you see noctilucent clouds? From what latitude? How late in twilight? (What is the solar depression angle?) How far from the summer solstice date?

2. What are the angular altitude, color, and structure of the clouds at different times during the display? What are the clouds' rate of motion?

97.

Aurora and Airglow

Look for traces of aurora and airglow on every suitable night. Study these phenomena in detail when you see them, but, first and foremost, learn how often they occur at your observing location.

The aurora, more popularly known in the Northern Hemisphere as the *Northern Lights,* can be perhaps the greatest of all the sky's "light shows"—that is to say, no phenomenon in the heavens can offer a greater variety of motion, form, and color.

Athough great displays of the aurora are rare at latitudes below 40 degrees or so, they do occur—especially in periods like the early 1990s. At that time, for a few years, the Sun will be reaching then declining from an unusually high peak in its roughly 11-year cycle of activity. On March 13, 1989, the aurora was seen as far south as Central America.

But our current activity is not concerned with the details of these most magnificent displays; it is instead concerned with perhaps the best of all ways to ensure you will not miss one. The activity is to watch your northern sky every possible night and become better at detecting all displays of the aurora, however weak. Along with all the intrinsic benefits of such an observational program, you thereby will also be improving scientific data on the frequency of the aurora—especially at lower latitudes.

One severe impediment is light pollution. Even if you observe in the country, cities many miles to your north can light up scattered clouds that can easily be mistaken for inactive auroral glows. Only experience in learning which is which will help.

Will there be enough auroral displays to be worth your effort? A viewer around 40 degrees north in the United States should be able to see the Northern Lights on about 5 percent of nights each year. Even down near Florida the figure is 1 percent—several nights of auroral displays per year. And these figures, if inaccurate, are likely to be too conservative.

Staying out frequently and knowing when you see the dim beginnings of an auroral display may also be the key to your seeing one of the grand outbreaks. Any would-be aurora watcher should also pay attention to solar activity. (Solar flares associated with large sunspot groups near the central meridian of the Sun's side facing us are our best bet for producing auroras.) You can keep track of solar

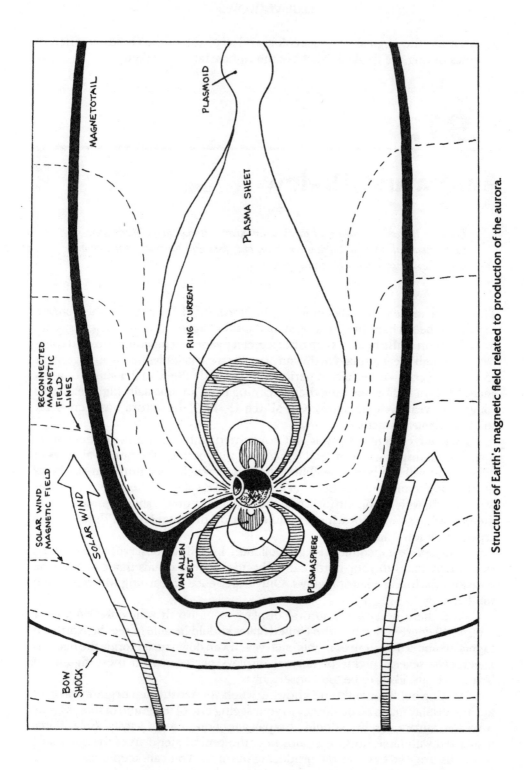

Structures of Earth's magnetic field related to production of the aurora.

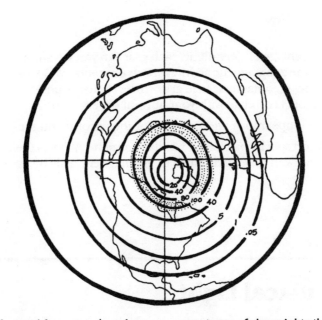

Map of auroral frequency (numbers are percentages of clear nights that aurora is visible).

activity in part by your own observations of the Sun (with a telescope and safe methods). Or listen to the shortwave radio station WWV (available on some less expensive radios like Radio Shack's Timecube) at 2.5, 5, 10, 15, or 20 megahertz, for one-day forecasts (at 18 minutes past each hour) of solar flares and geomagnetic activity. If you cannot pick up WWV, you can phone to hear the forecast on a recorded message from the Space Environment Services Center in Boulder, Colorado, (303) 497-3235. The k index (a measure of geomagnetic disturbance) at Boulder (about 40 degrees north) is also given, and updated every 3 hours. A k of 7 or more means a good aurora is then likely to be visible at least as far south as 40 degrees north.

You should also bear in mind that auroras are most likely to be seen at their most southerly in the middle of the night. If you spot only a patch of glow with no color and little or no movement, you may be uncertain. But if the amorphous glow fluctuates, better yet, forms into a horizontal arc, you know you are seeing the aurora.

Your nightly auroral searches may turn up the *airglow*. This glow is a kind of permanent aurora at certain wavelengths, which occurs predominantly in the lowest-altitude range of the aurora in the atmosphere. The airglow is always present, forming a major component of the light of the night sky, but on rather rare occasions, it is brighter in localized areas of the sky, visible as patches or bands. These could be safely identified as airglow when seen where only a major auroral display would reach or when other auroral activity is absent.

193

Questions

1. On what percentage of clear nights each year can you see auroras at your site? If you listen to the geomagnetic activity reports on station WWV or by phone, how do their ratings (geomagnetic field at storm levels active, unsettled, or quiet) and k index numbers correlate with your auroral observations?

2. What are the appearance and behavior of the auroras you see?

3. Can you detect special patches or bands of airglow? What is their appearance? Do they occur with any correlations to geomagnetic activity?

98.

The Zodiacal Light

Observe the zodiacal light, noting its prominence and extent on a number of nights.

The zodiacal light is a kind of tower or tilted pyramid of usually dim radiance seen in the west after evening twilight and the east after morning twilight. It is nothing more or less than light scattered from the Sun by countless micrometeoroidal particles in space.

The zodiacal light is best visible when the Zodiac (or the midline of the Zodiac, the *ecliptic*) makes a steep angle with the observer's horizon in the hour or two after evening twilight or before morning twilight. This is always more or less the case for observers in the tropics; but in north temperate latitudes (where most of the world's population lives), the ecliptic is only steep in the west after evening twilight around (actually a while before) the spring equinox and only steep in the east before morning twilight around (actually a while after) the autumn equinox. But this often-quoted restriction, and a reputation of being faint, ends up discouraging observation.

The object of this activity is not to just observe the zodiacal light as an oddity on one February evening or October morning a year—if you remember it during those months. Even if you are only going to try viewing it in the favorable periods of its steepness each year, view it on a number of nights.

One benefit of doing so is to permit comparison of its prominence on various nights and better comparison of it from season to season and year to year. Remembering to take into account atmospheric extinction, you can compare its glow with parts of the Milky Way—though sometimes the zodiacal light will be

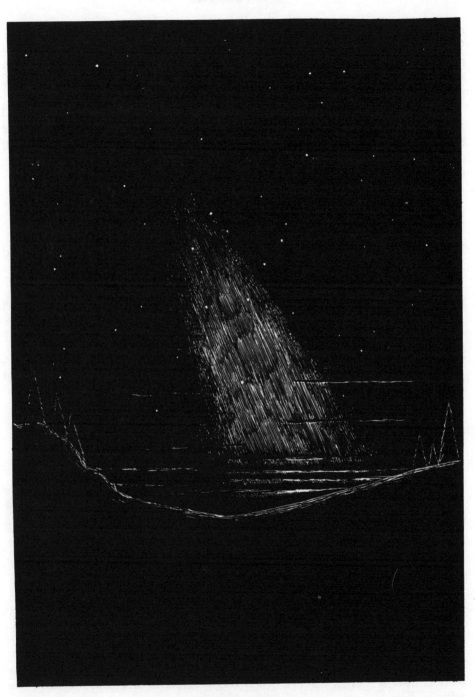

The zodiacal light.

much brighter than the winter Milky Way, which is up when the light is at its best. What would cause variations in the light's brightness? I have heard the argument that increased solar activity makes the zodiacal light brighter and the argument that increased airglow (stemming from increased solar activity?) makes it less prominent. See if you can form a conclusion from your own studies.

In addition to the brightness or prominence of the zodiacal light, you should also see how far along the Zodiac you can trace it. The zodiacal light under excellent conditions may be seen to extend for 30 to 40 degrees at the end of twilight. But under excellent conditions, an observer can trace a narrower extension of it all the way across the sky. (See the next activity.)

Questions

1. How often can you observe the zodiacal light after dusk or dawn in its seasonal periods of optimum visibility? How often (and how high and well) at other times of year?

2. How does the zodiacal light's brightness compare with that of various sections of the Milky Way? Does haze affect the visibility of one more than the other? How does their appearance differ? Can you detect color in the zodiacal light?

3. After you have factored out the variables of weather, duration of twilight, and altitude, how much does the true brightness of the zodiacal light vary from night to night, season to season, year to year? What do any variations seem correlated with—solar activity?

99.

Gegenschein and Zodiacal Band

Under excellent sky conditions, try to observe the gegenschein (or counterglow) and the zodiacal band (or light bridge). Record the size, position, and brightness of what you see plus the conditions under which you were observing.

The previous activity stated that the zodiacal light could, in excellent conditions, be seen to have a narrow extension that followed the Zodiac (or its midline, the ecliptic) all the way across the sky. The object of the current activity is to observe and study this *zodiacal band*, or *light bridge*, and the slight brightening of it that occurs at the anti-solar point in the night heavens—the *gegenschein*, or *counterglow*.

The gegenschein is the more famous of these phenomena, but much of its reputation stems from its supposed faintness. Dim it is, and yet in very dark and clear skies, its light is bright enough to be seen by anyone who knows where to look. Actually it may be better not to know exactly where along the ecliptic to look, so that, afterward, you can calculate where the anti-solar point was (180 degrees away from the Sun). You will certainly need averted vision. What you will be looking for is a diffuse patch roughly several degrees wide. When you see this counterglow, you are actually observing countless little micrometeoroids acting just like minute Full Moons shining back the Sun's light to Earth.

Observations of the gegenschein naturally cannot be made if the Moon itself is anywhere above the horizon. And it is best to have the gegenschein as high as possible—around the middle of the night and in Gemini in January. But other periods when the gegenschein cannot be seen are in December and June—because these are the times when the gegenschein is passing in front of the Milky Way, which is far brighter.

Actually, given an excellent dark sky, the observer may find it more often convenient to look for the zodiacal band, or light bridge. Although it is fainter than the gegenschein, I know from personal experience that it does not require a wilderness sky or the clearest night of your life to perceive it. You may be able to trace it most of the way across the sky—or at least along a high section of the Zodiac.

Questions

1. Can you spot the gegenschein? How faint does the limiting magnitude for stars at the zenith and in the gegenschein's vicinity have to be before it is visible? Do you find that the brightness of the gegenschein may vary from night to night or over longer periods? How large an extent of it can you see?

2. Can you detect the zodiacal band? How much of it can you trace across the sky? How faint does the limiting magnitude for stars at the zenith and stars in the band's vicinity have to be before it is visible?

100.

The Cloud Satellites of Earth

Look for the Kordylewski clouds, the cloud satellites of Earth.

In 1772, Joseph Louis Lagrange pointed out that, when one body orbits another, there will be in the plane of that orbit five stable *libration points* at which bodies of

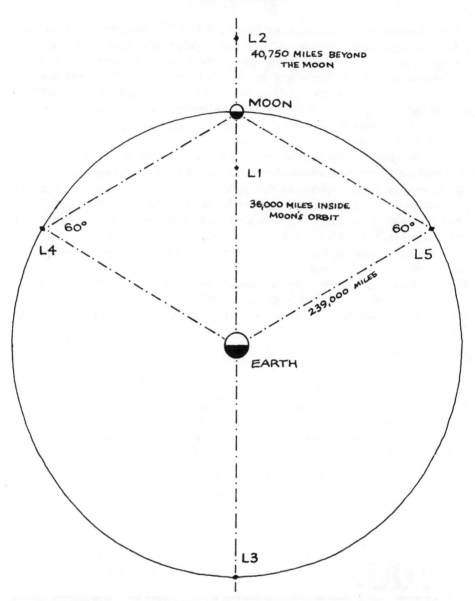

Figure 18 Libration points of the Earth-Moon system (sizes and distances not all to scale).

comparatively negligible mass could also orbit. Figure 18 shows the five positions for the Earth-Moon system, which may be of considerable interest for space colonists in our future. Actually it was the Sun-Jupiter system that was first proven to have bodies in the L_4 and L_5 points. These points form equilateral triangles with Jupiter and the Sun. Located at the points are the so-called *Trojan asteroids*—some of them forever about 60 degrees ahead of Jupiter in its orbit, some of them forever about 60 degrees behind Jupiter in its orbit.

Not until the 1950s did anyone seriously investigate the possibility that Earth might have additional moons in the L_4 and L_5 positions of the Earth-Moon system. The Polish astronomer K. Kordylewski began the search of these points with a telescope in 1951, but he came up empty-handed for years until a colleague made an important point. Perhaps the moons at these points might in fact be clouds of small particles, only visible with the superb capability for perceiving extended glows, which is possessed by an optical instrument known as . . . the naked eye.

In October 1956, Kordylewski succeeded with his naked eyes. There was indeed a cloud satellite of Earth at one of the positions, and, later, one was also found at the other position. In his first observation, Kordylewski reported that the cloud was about 2 degrees across and only about half as bright as the gegenschein. But the clouds may vary somewhat in extent and configuration.

Extremely few people have yet seen the cloud satellites of Earth. The clouds must be brightest when their little component particles are opposite the Sun from the Earth—at their Full phase. But this is only a few days away from when the Moon itself is Full and shining brightly all night. The best time to look for L_5 should be from about 3 to 5 days after full moon, maybe 3 or 4 hours after sunset, just before moonrise. Its position would be about 60 degrees west from the Moon on the Moon's current path through the sky (it changes each month), which is not quite the same as 60 degrees west on the ecliptic. And, just as with the gegenschein, there are the times when this position lies in the Milky Way, against which the L_5 cloud's feeble brightness would be utterly lost. Plus you would want the cloud in a high part of the Zodiac, to minimize atmospheric extinction as much as possible.

The requirements for the L_4, which we might call the *morning cloud*, complement those of L_5 in the morning sky—several days *before* full moon and just after moonset.

Incidentally, in the 1980s, spacecraft discovered that several moons of Saturn have smaller single (not cloud) moons preceding and/or following them at the Lagrangian points in their orbits.

Questions

1. Can you succeed in seeing one or both of the cloud satellites of Earth? What is their appearance, especially in their size and (compared to the gegenschein) their brightness?

2. At what time of night, month, and year do you see one of these clouds? What is the limiting magnitude of stars at the zenith and in the vicinity of the cloud when you see it?

Glossary

The entries that state "*See* Note. . ." refer to the "Note on the Measurement of Time, Position, Angular Distances, and Brightness in Astronomy."

Airglow: A permanent general glow emitted by certain atoms and molecules high in the atmosphere, ultimately caused by solar radiation, but not confined to polar regions as the aurora usually is

Albedo: The reflectivity of astronomical objects

Anti-solar point: The spot 180 degrees away from the Sun, thus not only in the opposite direction but as far below the horizon as the Sun is above (or vice versa)

Apogee: Far point of an orbit around Earth (opposite of *perigee*)

Apparition: Period of a planet's (or other object's) visibility between two periods when it is not viewable

Asterism: A pattern of stars that does not make up an official constellation

Atmospheric extinction: Dimming effect of air on a celestial light source

Aureole: The innermost area of scattered light around the Sun in our sky

Aurora: Formations of radiance produced usually in an oval around Earth's polar regions (*aurora borealis*—Northern Lights; *aurora australis*—Southern Lights) when upper-atmospheric gases are bombarded by energetic solar particles accelerated by Earth's magnetic field

Azimuth: Angular measure around the horizon or parallel to it in the sky (0 degrees usually considered North, 90 degrees, East, and so on)

Baily's Beads: Beads of the Sun's brilliant surface shining through lowland areas on the Moon's edge at start or end of a total solar eclipse

"Belt of Venus": Pinkish upper border to the earthshadow

Bishop's Ring: A special kind of huge corona, pale silver-blue surrounded by a pale brownish border, visible around the Sun only on rare occasions when sufficient concentration of tiny volcanic ash or aerosols is present in the atmosphere

Bolide: An exploding meteor

Celestial sphere: The imaginary sphere surrounding Earth, whose inner surface is the sky above and below one's horizon

Chinese lantern sun: A particular kind of distorted appearance of the low Sun caused by unusual refraction in the lower atmosphere

Chromosphere: A colorful layer of the Sun's atmosphere glimpsed briefly at the start and end of a total solar eclipse

Circumpolar: Circling close enough around the north or south celestial pole in the sky so as to never set as seen from certain locations on Earth

Coma (of a comet): The cloud of gas and dust surrounding an active comet's *nucleus,* and with the nucleus forming the comet's *head*

Comet: A mass of frozen gas and dust (the nucleus), which releases that gas and dust to form a *coma* and (generally) a *tail* when exposed to sufficient solar radiation and heating

Conjunction: Strictly speaking, the arrangement when one celestial object moves to a position due north or south of another; more loosely, any close pairing of celestial objects brought about by the motion of one or both

Constellation: An official pattern of stars, or, more strictly, the officially demarcated section of sky in which that pattern lies

Corona (caused by particles in clouds): One or more disks or bands of blue or green light, each bounded by a red band, seen around the Moon or Sun when cloud droplets or ice needles diffract the moonlight or sunlight

Corona (solar): The pearly white outer atmosphere of the Sun visible during total solar eclipses

Countersun: A mirage image of the Sun, which seems to rise to meet the real setting Sun (or detach to set away from the rising Sun) when there are certain conditions of refraction in the lower atmosphere

Crepuscular rays: Strips of shadow from distant clouds seen radiated from the departed Sun's position during twilight; their counterparts in the opposite sky are *anticrepuscular rays*

Culmination: The high point a celestial object reaches in its nightly voyage across the sky when it comes to the *meridian*

Cyanometer: A device for measuring the blue of the sky, consisting of a scale formed by swatches or patches of various shades of blue

Danjon scale: A scale consisting of verbal descriptions for estimating the brightness of total lunar eclipses; invented by A. Danjon

Dark adaptation: Increase in the eye's sensitivity to light, which occurs mostly in the first 15 to 30 minutes in a dark environment

Deep-sky objects: Astronomical objects beyond our solar system (usually refers to star clusters, nebulas and galaxies, less often to double stars and rarely to individual stars)

Diamond-ring effect: The appearance at the start and end of some total solar eclipses of a first starlike point of the Sun's surface seen through a valley on the Moon's edge like a diamond on the band of the still-visible solar corona

Diffraction: Process in which particles near to the size of the wavelengths of light (or other forms of electromagnetic radiation) interfere with the waves so as to produce brighter and darker zones

Double star: A star which, upon closer or further observation, turns out to consist of two or more component stars, either gravitationally bound to each other (true *binary system*) or appearing near to each other in the sky because on the same line of sight (*optical double*)

Earthshadow: The shadow of our planet seen projected on our atmosphere in the form of a segment in the sky opposite from where the Sun has just set or is just about to rise

Earthshine: The glow from the sunlit parts of Earth seen on the night part of the Moon

Eclipse: The hiding or dimming of one celestial object by another object or the other object's shadow

Ecliptic: The apparent path of the Sun through the Zodiac constellations, really the projection of Earth's orbit in the sky

Elongation: The angular separation of a celestial object from the Sun (rarely, Moon or other body) in the sky

Fireball: A meteor brighter than even the planet Venus

Galaxy: Vast congregation of many millions or billions of stars in elliptical, spiral, or irregular formation

Gegenschein: The slight brightening at the anti-solar point in the night sky caused by (mostly) micrometeoroidal particles presenting fully lit faces toward Earth

Glory: Pattern of rings of blue or green bounded by red around the anti-solar point in the day sky caused partly by diffraction from small particles (generally cloud droplets)

Green flash: The last (or first) speck of the Sun on the horizon appearing as a brief "star" of green due to differences in the refraction and absorption by our atmosphere of the various colors in sunlight

Halo phenomena: A large class of circles, arcs, pillars, and patches of sometimes colorful light in the sky produced by refraction and reflection of sunlight or moonlight by ice crystals, usually in cirrus and cirrostratus clouds (includes 22-degree halo, mock suns— also called sun dogs, or parhelia—and many other effects)

Heliacal rising: A celestial's first seasonal visibility at dawn (or, if *heliacal setting*, its last, at dusk)

Interference: The *destructive* or *constructive* reinforcement of light waves' peaks or troughs—creating zones of light and dark—caused by particles of nearly the same size as those waves

Inferior conjunction: Position in which an *inferior* planet (closer to the Sun than Earth is) passes the line between Sun and Earth (*See also superior conjunction*)

Iridescent clouds: Clouds displaying parts of corona bands of color, usually fairly near the Sun

Isocyans and isophotes: Lines of equal blueness and equal brightness, respectively (identical in blue-sky measurements)

Kordylewski clouds: The clouds of particles orbiting Earth at two of the libration points of the Earth-Moon system

Libration: Various kinds of tiltings of the face of the Moon pointed towards Earth

Libration points: The *L-points* at which very small objects can have stable orbit in relation to two much more massive bodies (like the Earth and Moon or the Sun and Jupiter)

Light pollution: Excessive or misdirected lighting (generally manmade and outdoor)

Limiting magnitude: The faintest magnitude (level of brightness) at which celestial objects (usually stars) can be seen with a given set of sky conditions and optical instrument (including the naked eye)

Limb: The edge of a celestial body like the Sun or Moon

Lunation: The period from one New Moon to the next New Moon

Magnitude: *See* "Note on the Measurement of Time, Angular Distances, and Brightness in Astronomy"

Mare (plural maria): The gray plains of ancient lava on the Moon

Meridian: The imaginary line from due north to overhead to due south in the sky

Meteor: A *shooting star;* actually, the streak of light produced when a piece of rock or iron from space (where it is called a *meteoroid*) burns up from friction in the atmosphere on its way to vaporization or (in rare cases) reaching the ground to becomes a *meteorite*

Meteoroid stream: A concentration of meteoroids around a particular orbit in space

Meteor shower: An increased number of meteors seeming to come from a particular point in the heavens (if very intense, a *meteor storm*)

Minutes of arc: *See* "Note . . ."

Moon Illusion: Optical illusion in which the low Moon looks large

Nacreous clouds: Special, very high-altitude iridescent clouds (also called *mother-of-pearl clouds*)

Nebula: A cloud of gas or dust in space among or around the stars. (Major kinds—diffuse, planetary, and dark nebulas)

Noctilucent clouds: Highest of all clouds, probably composed of micrometeorite dust and ice

Oblateness: Quality of having greater equatorial than polar width

Occultation: The hiding of one celestial object by another (a *grazing occultation* is one in which the uneven edge of one body alternately hides and reveals the other)

Old moon: The Moon extremely soon before New Moon

Opposition: Position opposite the Sun in the heavens

Penumbra: Lighter, peripheral shadow (usually of Earth)

Perigee: Near point of an orbit around Earth (opposite *apogee*)

Primary (twilight) glow: Twilight glow resulting from first scattering of sunlight by atmosphere and atmospheric particles

GLOSSARY

Purkinje effect: Result of the eye's greater sensitivity to shorter wavelengths at dimmer illumination levels

"Purple light": Secondary twilight glow appearing partway up the sky above the Sun's location when it is about 3 to 6 degrees below the horizon; rarely, followed by *counter purple light* and *second purple light*

Radiant: Area of the heavens from which a meteor shower radiates

Rays (on the Moon): Streaks of light-colored material ejected from craters on the Moon

Refraction: The bending of light rays which occurs when they pass from one medium to another, or through different densities of the same medium

Retrograde motion: Apparent backwards (westward) movement of planets in front of the starry background (opposite of *direct motion*)

Right ascension (RA): *See* "Note . . ."

Rills: Long cracklike features, often ravines, on the Moon

Seconds of arc: *See* "Note . . ."

"Seeing": Quality of astronomical images as a function of atmospheric turbulence

Shadow bands: Strips of moving shadow on the landscape, caused by a thin crescent Sun twinkling just before or after total solar eclipse

Sidereal month: The period required for the Moon to make one circuit around Earth and return to the same point as seen against the stars

Skyglow: Illumination of the sky by terrestrial sources (almost always manmade source, usually cities)

Solar depression angle (s.d.a.): Angle of the Sun below horizon

Spectre of the Brocken: *Glory* around the shadow of one's head seen on fog in the mountains

Sporadic meteor: A meteor not belonging to any known shower

Stationary point: Point at which a planet halts apparent motion in the heavens when switching from direct to retrograde motion (or back)

Sun-picture: A projected image of the Sun

Superior conjunction: Position in which an *inferior* planet (closer to the Sun than Earth is) passes the extension of the Sun-Earth line on the far side of the Sun from Earth (*see also inferior conjunction*)

Supernumerary arcs: The extra bands of color sometimes appearing just below the primary or (rarely) just above the secondary rainbow

Synodic month: The period required for the Moon to go from one phase to next recurrence of that phase (same Sun-Earth-Moon relation)

Tangent point: Point where the Sun's rays, which eventually pass into the atmosphere above an observer, are tangent to Earth's surface

Terminator: The line separating day and night on a world

Transparency: Quality of the atmosphere's ability to pass amount of light (in other words, clarity of the air)

Twilight: Period between day and night

Umbra: The central, darker shadow of any object, especially Earth

Young moon: The Moon extremely soon after New Moon

Zenith: The overhead point in the sky

Zodiac: The band of constellations in which the Sun, Moon, and planets are found and whose mid-line is the *ecliptic*

Zodiacal band: Very faint extension of the zodiacal light around the entire rest of the Zodiac

Zodiacal light: Roughly pyramid-shaped glow beyond twilight along zodiac, caused by forward-scattering of sunlight off (mostly) micrometeoroids in space

Selected Reading List

Books

Ashbrook, Joseph. *The Astronomical Scrapbook.* Cambridge, MA: Sky Publishing Corporation. Mostly astronomy history (fascinating) but also some wonderful facts and ideas for naked-eye observing projects.

Burnham, Jr., Robert. *Burnham's Celestial Handbook* (3 volumes). New York: Dover Publications, Inc. Primarily handbook of objects for telescopic observers but great wealth of information on naked-eye objects and star and constellation lore, plus introduction to astronomy and observing.

Crawford, David. *Light Pollution.* International Dark-sky Association, 3545 North Stewart, Tucson, AZ 85716. Large booklet (Crawford is now working on a full-length book on light pollution for Cambridge University Press).

Greenler, Robert. *Rainbows, Halos, and Glories.* New York: Cambridge University Press.

MacRobert, Alan. *Backyard Astronomy* and *More Backyard Astronomy* (Write for Sky Publishing Catalogue for information on "Backyard Package".) Cambridge, MA: Sky Publishing Corporation.

Mayall, R. Newton, Margaret Mayall, and Jerome Wyckoff. *The Sky Observer's Guide.* New York: Golden Press. A good introduction.

Meeus, Jean. *Astronomical Tables of the Sun, Moon, and Planets.* Willmann-Bell, Inc., P.O. Box 3125, Richmond, VA 23235.

Meinel, Aden, and Marjorie Meinel. *Sunsets, Twilights, and Evening Skies.* New York: Cambridge University Press.

Minnaert, Marcel. *The Nature of Light and Color in the Open Air.* New York: Dover Publications, Inc. Rainbows, halos, and hundreds of other atmospheric optics phenomena and projects.

Moore, Patrick. *New Guide to the Moon.* New York: W. W. Norton & Company, Inc.

Norton's 2000.0 Star Atlas and Reference Handbook. Ian Ridpath, editor. New updated version of the classic naked-eye star atlas and excellent reference handbook. Longman Scientific & Technical and John Wiley & Sons, Inc. (New York).

Ottewell, Guy. *The Astronomical Companion.* Astronomical Workshop, Department of Physics, Furman University, Greenville, SC 29613. An atlas-sized astronomy handbook with inventive diagrams and peerlessly thorough and clear explanations.

_____ and Fred Schaaf. *Mankind's Comet.* Astronomical Workshop (see address above). Most comprehensive work on Halley's Comet. Still useful for Halley history, future projections, and information on comets and comet observing.

Raymo, Chet. *365 Starry Nights.* Englewood Cliffs, NJ: Prentice Hall. Enlightening observing activities for every night of the year, presented with delight and vigor.

Roggemans, Paul, editor. *Handbook for Visual Meteor Observations.* Cambridge, MA: Sky Publishing Corporation. Somewhat technical but invaluable guide for meteor watchers.

Schaaf, Fred. *The Starry Room.* New York: John Wiley & Sons, Inc. Collection of essays providing information on eclipses, meteors, comets, light pollution, conjunctions, naked-eye observing techniques, and other topics.

_____. *Wonders of the Sky.* New York: Dover Publications, Inc. Introduction to naked-eye astronomy.

Periodicals

Astronomy. Kalmbach Publishing Co. Monthly general astronomy magazine.

International Dark-sky Association Newsletter. See address for Crawford booklet above. Quarterly report on light pollution news.

Meteor News. Route 3, Box 1062, Callahan, FL 32011. Quarterly on meteor shower prospects and results; other information on meteors and meteorites.

SEAN (Scientific Event Alert Network) *Bulletin.* National Museum of Natural History, Mail Stop 129, Washington, DC 20560. Monthly reports on bright meteors and meteorites.

Sky & Telescope. Sky Publishing Corporation. Monthly general astronomy magazine.

Sky Calendar. Abrams Planetarium, Michigan State University, East Lansing, MI 48824. Monthly sheet (sent quarterly in packs of three) giving concise diagrams and information on what is visible in the heavens.

Annual

Astronomical Calendar. By Guy Ottewell. Astronomical Workshop (see address under Ottewell book above). Marvelous atlas-size guide to the year's events in the sky. Packed with information and unique helpful diagrams.

Maps, Audiovisual Aids, and Other Educational Materials

Astronomical Society of the Pacific. 390 Ashton Avenue, San Francisco, CA 94112. Photographs, slide-sets, video- and audiotapes, plus books and magazine *Mercury.*

Sky Publishing Corporation. (See address under Ashbrook book above.) Among many other publications, lunar and planetary maps and ESSCO classroom publications (including Laboratory Exercises in Astronomy).

Index

209